OXFORD NEUROLOGICAL MONOGRAPHS

EDITED BY
W. RITCHIE RUSSELL

THE
TRAUMATIC
AMNESIAS

BY

W. RITCHIE RUSSELL

C.B.E., M.D. (Edin.), D.Sc. (Oxon.), F.R.C.P. (Edin. and Lond.)

Formerly Professor of Clinical Neurology,
University of Oxford
Consultant Neurologist to the British Army
and to the Ministry of Pensions

OXFORD UNIVERSITY PRESS

1971

Oxford University Press, Ely House, London W.1

GLASGOW   NEW YORK   TORONTO   MELBOURNE   WELLINGTON
CAPE TOWN   SALISBURY   IBADAN   NAIROBI   DAR ES SALAAM   LUSAKA   ADDIS ABABA
BOMBAY   CALCUTTA   MADRAS   KARACHI   LAHORE   DACCA
KUALA LUMPUR   SINGAPORE   HONG KONG   TOKYO

PRINTED IN GREAT BRITAIN
AT THE PITMAN PRESS BATH

PREFACE

DURING the past forty years, the author and his associates have been studying the effects of various types of head injury and these have been presented in over twenty publications. In all these the traumatic amnesias have provided one of the central features for study, and it has been suggested that a collection of these studies would now be useful, for the subject continues to be of special interest to those who study the physiology of brain mechanisms. This volume presents, with a commentary, numerous extracts from papers written by the author and his associates between the years 1932 and 1969.

The nineteen papers listed here are those that have been particularly concerned with the traumatic amnesias. Those from which extracts have been reprinted in this volume are marked with an asterisk.

1. Brain involvement in head injury (1932). *Edinb. med. J.* **39**, 25–36.
*2. Cerebral involvement in head injury (1932). *Brain* **55**, 549–603.
*3. The after-effects of head injury (1934). *Edinb. med. J.* **41**, 129–41.
*4. Amnesia following head injuries (1935). *Lancet* **2**, 762–3.
5. Experimental cerebral concussion (1941) (with D. Denny-Brown). *Brain* **64**, 93–164.
*6. Accidental head injuries (1943) (with C. P. Symonds). *Lancet* **1**, 7–9.
*7. Traumatic amnesia (1946) (with P. W. Nathan). *Brain* **69**, 280–300.
8. The neurology of brain wounds (1947). *Br. J. Surg., War Surg. Supplement No. 1.*
9. Traumatic amnesia (1948). *Q. Jl exp. Psychol.* **1**, 1–4.
*10. Studies in amnesia (1948). *Edinb. med. J.* **55**, 92–9.
*11. Crushing injuries to the skull (1949) (with F. Schiller). *J. Neurol. Neurosurg. Psychiat.* **12**, 52–8.
12. Disability caused by brain wounds (1951). *J. Neurol. Neurosurg. Psychiat.* **14**, 35–9.
*13. The physiology of memory (1958). *Proc. R. Soc. Med.* **51**, 9–15.
*14. *Brain: memory: learning* (1959). Clarendon Press, Oxford.
15. *Traumatic aphasia* (1961) (with M. L. E. Espir). Clarendon Press, Oxford.
*16. Post-traumatic amnesia in closed head injury (1961) (with Aaron Smith). *Archs Neurol., Chicago* **5**, 4-17.
*17. Amnésie de mémoration caused by brain wounds (1963). *Trans. Am. neurol. Ass.* pp. 43–4.
18. *Aspects of learning and memory* (1966) (Edited by D. Richter). Chapter with F. Newcombe, p. 15. Heinemann, London.
*19. *Biochemical aspects of neurological disorders* (1968), Chapter 11. Blackwell Scientific Publications, Oxford.

Special thanks are due to Sir Charles Symonds, Dr. Peter Nathan, Professor Aaron Smith, and Dr. M. L. E. Espir for permission to quote from joint publications; to the editors and publishers of the following journals, who have allowed the reproduction of papers: *Brain, Lancet, Quarterly Journal of Experimental Psychology, Journal of Neurology, Neurosurgery and Psychiatry, Proceedings of the Royal Society of Medicine, Archives of Neurology, Edinburgh Medical Journal, Transactions of the American Neurological Association;* and to Messrs. Blackwell Scientific Publications Ltd. and William Heinemann Medical Books Ltd. for permission to reproduce extracts from books published by them.

Ever since 1930, and particularly during World War II, support has been received from the Medical Research Council. The Nuffield Provincial Hospitals Trust, the National Fund for Research into Crippling Diseases, the Michael Maxwell Memorial Fund, other charitable bodies and private benefactors have also made these studies possible.

I am especially indebted to Sir Charles Symonds and Dr. Freda Newcombe for scrutinizing the manuscript and suggesting many corrections and improvements.

CONTENTS

INTRODUCTION

THE effects of head injury on the mechanisms of remembering are of both academic and practical importance. The process of being fully orientated and capable of correlating one event with the next requires that the sequence of events be remembered at least for a considerable time: for this to happen it seems necessary to assume a high grade of normal behaviour by the brain. Thus it is a commonplace occurrence that serious illnesses, injuries, and intoxications cause an illness that upsets this mechanism so that the illness may not be subsequently remembered by the patient. During the period of confusion in such an illness there may be some memories or hallucinations, indicating that both the mechanism of storing information and of recalling previous experience is distorted.

The average case of accidental head injury involves subjecting the brain to a sudden jolt and the most commonplace feature of accidental head injury is some disturbance of consciousness, so that the patient may be 'knocked out' by his experience.

The term 'a sudden jolt to the brain' refers to a very sudden change of velocity such as occurs when a moving head strikes a hard surface in a fall, or when a rapidly moving object strikes the head and subjects it to a high velocity from being stationary. This change of velocity in head injury occurs very rapidly and therefore involves for a few milliseconds some very high accelerations to the skull to the extent of some hundreds g—in other words some thousands of feet per second. From the point of view of dynamics there is no difference between the accelerations involved in the head while moving striking a stationary object, and the head while stationary being hit by a large, rapidly moving object, for the two are similar as far as the relevant physics is concerned.

Experimental studies of what happens when the brain is subjected to a rapid change of velocity of this kind indicate that, as might be expected on theoretical grounds, the pressures rise at the site of impact and fall away to a negative phase at the site opposite the place at which the skull is struck; this leads to extensive movement of one part of the brain on another which is so severe, and so obvious in experimental work, that this commotion and distortion of the centre of the cerebral hemispheres seems to be the basis of the disturbed brain function that is evident by the sudden loss of consciousness.

This is the mechanism by which brain damage occurs in the ordinary type of accidental closed head injury—*acceleration concussion* (Denny-Brown and Russell 1941)—and it is in relation to this background that many aspects of the traumatic amnesias must be considered.

I

THE IMMEDIATE EFFECTS OF CEREBRAL ACCELERATION CONCUSSION

THE immediate effects of concussion are usually that the individual drops to the ground motionless, often with an arrest of respiration, and at this stage basic reflexes such as the corneal response may be abolished. After respiration returns, restless movements appear and by very gradual stages the patient begins to speak, resist interference, make a noise, and becomes restless, talkative, abusive, and irritable in one way or another. Slowly his speech becomes more intelligible and then as the effect of the trauma wears off he looks around wondering where he is: the period of traumatic confusion is at an end, but he has no recollection of any event that occurred since the injury. Further, there is a short period before the injury that he does not remember—the so-called period of retrograde amnesia (R.A.).

A remarkable feature of the traumatic coma, stupor, and confusion that follow acceleration concussion is that its duration seems to be infinitely variable in that, although the stages of recovery may be much the same from one patient to another, the time taken for the recovery to occur varies widely from a few minutes to a few hours, a few days, or a few weeks, while in a few instances recovery never occurs, and a permanent state of dementia and helplessness results.

The likelihood is that all these experiences represent varying degrees of a similar process which in the mild situation results from the effects of a general twisting and displacement of fibre tracts in the brain one on another, but in the severe cases results in not only a distortion of these tracts, but in widespread tearing of their fibres, such as have been described by Strich (1956) and Oppenheimer (1968). There seems therefore to be a difference in degree only between the mild cerebral concussion from which a complete recovery occurs within a few hours, and the disastrous grade of trauma that produces permanent destruction of white matter throughout the cerebral hemispheres.

There was at one time an attempt to grade cases of acceleration concussion into concussion, contusion, laceration, and compression by haemorrhage, but this type of classification cannot now be accepted as satisfactory, for these changes refer to naked-eye appearances of the brain at operation or at post mortem examination, and bear little relationship to the gross microscopic anomalies in nerve-fibre integrity within the white matter of the cerebral hemispheres. These can now be shown by special techniques to occur widely without there being any visible naked-eye evidence of such damage. We are therefore faced with the problem of classification and, as far as closed accidental concussion of the acceleration type is concerned, it is simpler basically to look on all cases as being different grades of the one type of trauma caused by violent accelerations. For convenience it is probably easiest to use the term 'acceleration concussion' to describe all varieties, but then some indication must be given of severity and, of course, of complications such as intra-cerebral haemorrhage, gross areas of brain contusion, etc.

Another reason for looking at all these cases as being the same is the question of the time taken for the abnormal effects of cerebral concussion to wear off, which varies so widely. Here we encounter an interesting phenomenon in relation to trauma to the nervous system, whether it be to the head, the spinal cord, or the peripheral nerve; the severity of trauma, short of severing the part of nervous system concerned, seems to be reflected closely by the time taken for recovery to occur. There must, therefore, be some inherent characteristics by which trauma to individual neurones or groups of neurones recovers on a time-scale dependent on the distorting effect of the injury. This is relevant to the question of amnesia in relation to cerebral concussion, for obviously a head injury that causes disturbed consciousness for 5 minutes is less severe than one that causes disturbance of consciousness for 5 days, and the duration of disturbed consciousness therefore provides some indication of the severity of the uncomplicated case of closed head injury.

During recovery the patient is at one stage obviously unconscious, but he may pass later through a stage of recovery in which his behaviour is relatively normal, although he is still slightly confused, and is unable to recall events from moment to moment, so that subsequently he cannot remember what he has said during these later stages of his mental recovery. Indeed, a good indication of full recovery of consciousness seems to be a return of normal orientation, full awareness of the sequence of events, and an ability to store events so that what happens can be recalled at a later date. This is fortunate, for after recovery the patient can often give a clear indication of when he became aware of his surroundings after the injury, and the duration of amnesia following the injury—the post-traumatic amnesia (P.T.A.) as it is now called—gives a fair indication of the duration of disturbed consciousness, and thus often provides a valuable indication of the severity of the injury.

The studies reported in paper 2 were made during the years 1930 and 1931. At this time there were a number of existing views regarding the mechanisms of head injury and their complications which cause considerable confusion. In the first place, there was the strongly held view that concussion was due to the blood being squeezed out of the brain; and secondly there was almost an obsession with the view that swelling of the brain was the main cause of all complications and that 'unresolved contusion' was the cause of head injury after-effects. These views have now been abandoned but they had to be challenged at the time, as is apparent from the following extracts from paper 2 (Russell 1932).

The mechanism by which the brain is injured.—It is a remarkable fact that the skull, which contains a fragile structure such as the brain, can be subjected to sudden blows of considerable severity without injury to the brain, especially in view of the fact that some movement of the brain relative to the skull may occur as is evidenced by the occasional tearing of a cortical vein from its attachment to a venous sinus. Whether the head receives a blow or whether the head strikes the ground, the mechanism of cerebral injury is the same. The brain is obliged to undergo a sudden change in momentum, which, if the skull were not there to protect it, would cause its complete destruction. The fact that the brain fits the skull accurately is the main factor which enables the skull itself to bear the brunt of the blow.

The force applied to the skull in a case of concussion may be great and may be applied to only a small area of its surface. The force of the blow is, however, conveyed to the brain by the whole inner aspect of the skull on the side injured, and in this way is so distributed that the damage to any one part is correspondingly reduced.

Beyond violence of a certain degree, however, the brain also becomes damaged. Here again the effect is lessened by the force of the blow being distributed to all parts of the cerebrum. That a mechanism exists which distributes the strain to all parts, and so reduces the damage to any one part, is shown by the scattered capillary haemorrhages which are often found throughout the brain of cases in which no gross cerebral contusion can be demonstrated.

Contre-coup injury.—It is largely through the tearing of small vessels in the pia arachnoid that haemorrhage into the cerebrospinal fluid occurs. The bleeding is usually greatest at a point exactly opposite to that at which the injury is received. It seems that this so-called *contre-coup* injury, which is the most constant of all post-mortem findings in these cases, cannot be explained by any wave of force having been applied to the brain at that point. If we take, for example, the case of a man who falls on the frontal region on a hard surface, the momentum of the skull is arrested with great suddenness and the skull, in its turn, arrests the momentum of the brain in the manner described above. The force of the brain's momentum is directed towards making the brain continue its velocity in a downward (frontal in this case) direction. The occasional tearing of a cerebral vein provides conclusive evidence that some movement of the brain relative to the skull can take place. All parts of the brain are attempting to move in the same direction, and the maximum movement relative to the skull will be at a point opposite to the site of the frontal impact, viz., in the occipital region. It is I think apparent that the subarachnoid space is the place of least resistance to this force. The combined forces of surface tension and intracranial pressure will prevent the spaces between the dura mater and skull, or the dura mater and arachnoid, being opened up. What then are the forces which prevent the space between the pia mater and arachnoid being forced open? In the first place there is the intracranial pressure which is slightly greater than atmospheric pressure, and in the second place there are the fine fibrous bands uniting the pia mater and arachnoid. The former force is the most important, but is some-what lessened because, unlike the subdural space, it is possible for the subarachnoid space to enlarge without becoming a vacuum. This is because it can be filled with cerebrospinal fluid from other parts. Indeed the fact that brain tissue is heavier than the cerebrospinal fluid will tend to make the brain force itself downwards (forwards in this case) at the expense of the less heavy fluid, which will therefore tend to flow away from the site of impact.

Any such movement of the brain would be greatly lessened or abolished were the skull a closed box containing a constant volume of tissue and fluid. This doctrine of the skull being a closed box of this nature cannot, however, be accepted as correct; because in the first place, the volume of the brain can be greatly reduced by forcing blood away from it, and in the second place, the brain and cerebrospinal fluid have considerable room for expansion through the foramen magnum. I therefore suggest that the common *contre-coup* injury is caused by the brain tearing itself from its coverings by the force of its own momentum. The damage is therefore most likely to occur at that part of the brain which is opposite to the site of injury, though in very severe cases the injury may be much more extensive.

Should this be the correct explanation of the mechanisms by which *contre-coup* damage is produced, the type of injury found in this situation should be of a different nature to that found at the site of impact. This is precisely what actually occurs. At the site of injury some cerebral contusion may be apparent, the features of which are discoloration of the surface of the brain with small haemorrhages within its substance. Haemorrhage on the surface of the brain is, at the site of injury, absent or slight.

In the case of *contre-coup* injury, on the other hand, sub-arachnoid haemorrhage is the chief and often the only sign. The arachnoid may be lifted up from the surface of the brain by a collection of blood. Extensive haemorrhage may occur into the brain substance, but this is merely an extension of haemorrhage from the surface where the actual tearing of the vessels occurs. Examples of *contre-coup* injury are shown in figs. 6 and 7. The *contre-coup* damage usually appears to be much greater than the damage at the sight of injury, but this may be more apparent than real owing to its haemorrhagic nature.

Mechanism of loss of consciousness.—The sudden loss of consciousness at the time of injury is considered by Trotter (1924) to be due to cerebral anaemia caused by a sudden flattening of the skull, what he terms "Acute compressive anaemia". There are, however, difficulties in accepting this explanation. In the first place, the loss of consciousness is immediate and recovery is relatively slow. There are other conditions in which loss of consciousness is due to cerebral anaemia. Such may occur when a debilitated person suddenly assumes the erect posture. Loss of consciousness in this case is preceded by a feeling of lightheadedness which lasts for a second or two, and in contrast to what happens after concussion, recovery of consciousness occurs completely as soon as the position of the head relative to the heart is adjusted by a fall to the ground. Banking at corners in high-speed flying may produce the same effect, the blood being suddenly forced from the brain by its own momentum. In this case recovery of full consciousness occurs as soon as the sudden changing of direction is modified. A more prolonged period of cerebral anaemia occurs in a Stokes–Adams' seizure, in which the loss of consciousness is so prolonged that a convulsion often occurs, yet here again consciousness often returns as soon as the circulation is re-established. Further, the theory of an acute

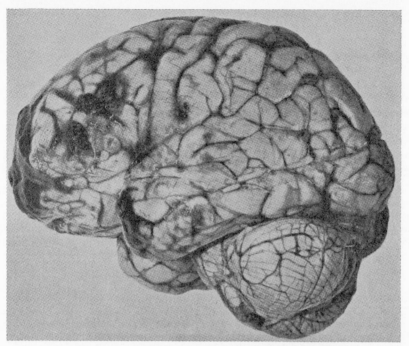

FIG. 6. *Contre-coup* injury, showing sub-arachnoid haemorrhage.

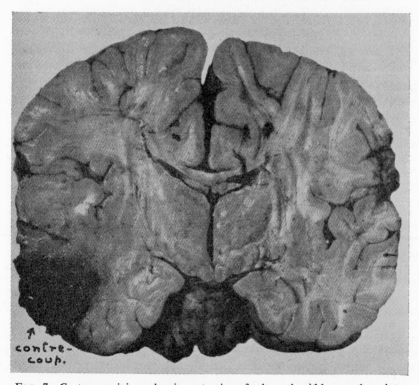

FIG. 7. *Contre-coup* injury, showing extension of sub-arachnoid haemorrhage into substance of the brain.

compressive anaemia does not explain why one patient should be unconscious for five and another for a period of thirty minutes. In the latter case, though the blow was presumably more severe, the duration of compression of the brain, should it have occurred, cannot have been of longer duration. Again, if loss of consciousness were due to cerebral anaemia, one would expect that in the very mild cases at least recovery of function would be rapid. We find on the contrary that recovery of full function of the brain, even in the slightest injuries, is always a relatively slow process. Even in the mildest cases of concussion, those in which the individual does not lose the power of either walking or speaking, he remains in a dazed state for several seconds, during which time he gradually recovers his full mental powers.

The following case is of particular interest in this connection:

W. R., a male, aged 34, had an accident while working in a mine on October 9, 1931. His head was crushed with considerable force between two hutches. This, however, did not cause him to lose consciousness immediately. He remembers all the details of the accident. He remembers sitting down after it occurred, while another worker bandaged his head. He remembers going up the pit shaft and entering the ambulance. Soon after entering the ambulance, however, he lost consciousness and did not regain his senses until in the Infirmary. When admitted, he had severe throbbing pains in his head. There was no visible fracture on X-ray examination and he was discharged a week later.

Soon after returning home he began to have "fainting turns" in which he would lose consciousness for a few seconds. No history of convulsions was obtained, but coincident with the onset of these turns pain in the head became severe and continued until he was admitted to Ward 32 under Professor Bramwell's charge on January 8, 1932. His complaint then was of severe and continual throbbing frontal pain and "fainting turns". He responded well to treatment with rest in bed and dehydration measures, and felt fit when discharged four weeks later.

In this case intracranial structures were sufficiently compressed and damaged to produce severe after-effects, yet no initial loss of consciousness occurred.

It would appear that the effect on the brain is not unlike the response of a peripheral nerve to an injury. Obstruction of all circulation to a nerve, as can be obtained by applying a sphygomomanometer armlet to the limb, fails to interrupt its functioning capacity except after many minutes. A sudden jar to the nerve trunk, however, causes an immediate interference with function, the severity and duration of which are directly proportional to the severity of the injury. Recovery of function is here, as in concussion, a relatively slow process. For these reasons it seems probable that the ancient conception of a commotion occurring in the nerve elements is the correct explanation of the sudden loss of consciousness. According to this view, the concussion of the nerve elements causes some molecular change which brings about a temporary interruption of function. That the myelin sheaths, at least, are easily disturbed by a sudden jar is demonstrated by the ease with which slight carelessness in removing a spinal cord at autopsy will alter the myelin sheaths sufficiently to enable them to be stained by Marchi's method.

As has already been shown, the force of the blow received by the skull is distributed to all parts of the brain. After a severe blow to the skull, therefore, all parts of the brain must suffer to a greater or less degree. It is therefore not surprising that the site of the injury is of little significance in most cases. From whatever angle the skull is jolted or struck, the whole of the brain receives a certain degree of jarring, its whole mechanism is put out of action, and consequently consciousness is immediately lost. Consciousness cannot exist unless the association paths within the cerebrum are acting normally; hence any temporary interruption of conduction in the intracerebral fibres will cause immediate loss of consciousness. My conception of the mechanism of concussion is, therefore, that at the moment of injury the whole of the brain tissue undergoes mechanical agitation. This causes molecular disturbance within the nerve elements (probably in the myelin sheaths) which brings about an interruption in the conducting functions of the nerve-cell processes, and leads to the instantaneous loss of consciousness.

Types of injury.—It is interesting to consider the different types of head injury from the point of view of the degree of jar, or agitation, which they cause to the brain.

The degree of injury to the skull and brain must depend on:

(1) Rapidity with which the momentum of the brain and skull is altered.

(2) The degree of change of momentum. The momentum of a body depends on its mass and its velocity. The mass of the skull and brain is approximately constant, therefore the degree of injury must depend on: (*a*) the rapidity with which the velocity is altered; (*b*) the amount of change of velocity.

If, for example, the patient falls from a height on to a stone surface, both the above factors contribute towards the occurrence of a serious degree of brain damage.

(1) The velocity of the skull is arrested with great suddenness at the moment of contact with the hard stone.

(2) The velocity of the skull which is high at the moment of impact is completely abolished and may actually become negative if the skull rebounds. Hence the degree of change of velocity is great.

If, instead of a fall on a stone surface, the patient falls on soft grass, the amount of change of velocity is the same, but the suddenness of change of velocity is much less owing to the softer surface. Hence the injury to the skull and brain is less severe.

Many cases have been described in the literature of the subject in which a pointed metal instrument has transfixed the skull and brain without consciousness being lost. This occurrence can be readily explained by the above conception. The point of the instrument being relatively sharp, a large part of its velocity is expended not in imparting velocity to the skull, but in penetrating its substance, and correspondingly the rapidity with which the skull is made to assume velocity is not inconsiderably lessened by this same factor. Any effort, so to speak, on the part of the instrument to impart a sudden velocity to the skull is prevented by the same effort causing further penetration of the skull by the metal instrument.

In the case of a moving object striking the head while at rest, the rapidity of the change of velocity of the skull and the degree of its change of velocity, depend on the momentum of the force which strikes it. As has already been mentioned, momentum depends on the two factors—the velocity of the object and the mass of the object. It therefore follows that a rapidly moving object and a heavy object, and especially one which possesses both these properties, will cause most damage to the brain.

Changes during recovery.—When consciousness is beginning to return and motor recovery has occurred, a stage of great restlessness and resistiveness is likely to supervene. This stage is often called the "stage of cerebral irritation" and is considered to be due to cerebral oedema, with a consequent increase of intracranial pressure. As has already been shown, however, the mental state is not in any way proportional to the pressure as estimated by the manometer; indeed, as already mentioned, seven stuporose cases which subsequently recovered showed a pressure within the limits of the normal. While the individual is very irritable in the popular sense of the word, there is no evidence that the condition is due to any mechanical irritation of the nervous elements. As Symonds (1932) has pointed out, other pathological conditions which cause cerebral oedema, such as cerebral tumour and uraemia, do not produce a clinical picture in any way resembling this traumatic state.

The condition is seen in all degrees of concussion. The concussed football player often moves his limbs restlessly and talks meaninglessly, and a few cases of head injury are violent and abusive when seen in the out-patient department. Though in slight injuries the duration of this stage is brief when compared to what may be seen in severe cases, it seems that the condition has the same significance in both types of case. In this stage of irritability, consciousness is not fully recovered and the patients have no subsequent recollection of their actions. It is probable that these irritable states merely represent a stage in the recovery of consciousness. The mental and other higher cerebral functions have not yet recovered, and owing to the lack of their control the more primitive and less vulnerable motor activity is running wild.

Oedema and other circulatory disturbances are frequent complications of cerebral trauma, and their far-reaching effects must not be lost sight of. It seems improbable, however, that they are the cause of the sudden loss of consciousness, or that they provide the explanation of the condition called cerebral irritation.

2

THE DURATION OF AMNESIA IN CLOSED HEAD INJURIES

IT is well known that a relatively slight bump on the head may render the victim dazed or knocked out for a few minutes, while more severe injuries, such as those caused by falls on a hard surface, may cause a dangerous degree of cerebral commotion with prolonged impairment of consciousness.

In the preceding chapter it has been postulated that the mechanisms involved in slight concussion and in severe cerebral commotion are fundamentally the same, in that the waves of distortion within the brain disturb performance in varying degrees. In severe injuries, of course, there is also an increased risk of complications, such as fractures of the skull or intracranial haemorrhage.

As all parts of the nervous system—brain, spinal cord, or peripheral nerve —show a close correlation between the severity of injury and the duration of the resulting disorder of function, there are therefore good reasons for considering this factor in relation to closed head injury. The simplest and most informative way of assessing the duration of disturbed brain function in cerebral commotion is to assess *the duration of loss of full consciousness*. This occurred in 200 consecutive cases admitted to Edinburgh Royal Infirmary during the year 1930 and reported in paper 2 (Russell 1932, extract from pp. 552–4).

In using this classification it is necessary to consider what are to be accepted as the criteria for full return of consciousness. The usual stages of recovery are somewhat similar in all degrees of injury, though the duration of the stages of recovery varies greatly. They may now be conveniently described.

Stages of recovery.—Immediately after the blow the whole of the nervous system may be paralysed; even the respiratory and cardiac movements may cease. If recovery is to occur, the heart and respiration recommence. Involuntary movements of the limbs then occur, and the reflexes return. Speech returns with a few words or phrases, and movements become more purposeful. Up to this stage it is mainly the lower mechanisms of the brain that are recovering, and the similarity between cases is great. The higher cerebral functions, however, differ in every individual, and the stages of recovery of these functions produce widely different clinical pictures. The mental condition may simulate any of the states seen in alcoholic poisoning; in both conditions the clinical picture probably depends on the individual psychological structure and balance. Thus the patient may be drowsy or talkative, docile or aggressive, impudent or irritable. He may tell you his secrets, may be boastful or affectionate, and may even attempt to bribe his attendants to let him out of bed.

Then, comparatively suddenly, he looks round and asks where he is. He has now recovered full consciousness and returns to this normal behaviour and treats those who are looking after him with the customary civility. These changes indicate that the higher functions of control and inhibition have again taken charge of his behaviour. These are the first to be affected in alcoholic poisoning and are the last to recover after a head injury. They presumably constitute the most sensitive mechanisms in the brain. These stages of recovery may be traced not only in the more severe cases, but also in those in which the individual is unconscious for a few minutes only.

It is sometimes difficult to determine at what stage consciousness has fully returned, and indeed in some severe cases the individual is never again able to carry out the same mental processes as were possible before the accident. In this series, the patient was not considered to have recovered full consciousness unless he was fully orientated and able to answer questions intelligently. He should, for example be able to describe clearly what he last remembered before the accident and what he first remembered after it. The victim of an accident may be able to move and even to talk sensibly and yet have no subsequent memory of his words or actions. This is a familiar state of affairs; as for example, when a football player is able to continue the game after a head injury and subsequently have no recollection of it. This failure to commit his actions to memory would indicate, according to the scheme here used, that he had not recovered consciousness in full. Such a patient may answer simple inquiries not unnaturally and yet be found on cross-examination to be disorientated as regards time and place. It is, therefore, apparent that *the evidence of untrained observers as to when full consciousness returns is of little value.* How then can this duration of unconsciousness be estimated? In the state of full consciousness any occurrence in which the patient is actively or passively concerned makes an impression on the memory, and can be subsequently called to mind. It has accordingly been found that the patient's subsequent memory of when he woke up provides a not inaccurate indication of when consciousness returned. By this indication, the duration of loss of consciousness can be estimated with fair accuracy even when the patient is seen for the first time long after the accident.

Grouping of Cases according to Duration of Loss of Consciousness

The cases of the series have been divided as follows:

Group "A" were unconscious for less than 1 hour . . . 80 cases
Group "B" were unconscious for from 1 to 24 hours . . . 57 cases
Group "C" were unconscious for more than 24 hours . . 47 cases
Group "D" comprised the fatal cases . . . . . 16 cases

Table IV shows that, after the age of 40, the percentage of fatal results rises greatly, and correspondingly the number of cases in Group C becomes proportionately much less than in the earlier years. This probably indicates that as age advances the individual becomes progressively less able to withstand the effects of severe injury, and this explanation is supported by the fact, as will be shown later, that full recovery of cerebral function after a head injury is much less likely to occur in the old than in the young.

TABLE IV.—*Table showing the Relation of the Age-Periods to the Degree of Cerebral Damage. The Proportion of Fatalities in each Age-Period is also shown*

Age-period	Group				Totals	Percentage died
	A	B	C	D		
0–10 years	10	2	10	1	23	4·4 per cent
10–20 years	19	13	6	1	39	2·6 per cent
20–30 years	20	18	18	2	58	3·4 per cent
30–40 years	8	10	5	1	24	4·2 per cent
40–50 years	13	6	3	3	25	12·0 per cent
50–60 years	6	1	1	3	11	27·0 per cent
60–70 years	3	6	1	4	14	28·6 per cen-
Over 70 years	1	1	3	1	6	16·7 per cent
Totals	80	57	47	16	200	8·0 per cent

Paper 3 (1934) reported a follow-up study of the cases studied in paper 2 and also compared the rate of recovery for full work (in working-class men and women) with the duration of P.T.A. The cases with a 'compensation factor' are those in which financial compensation for the injury is a factor requiring assessment in relation to duration of unfitness for work. Thus from paper 3 (Russell 1934, extract from pp. 135–6):

A fair indication of the severity of the cerebral injury can be obtained from the duration of the loss of full consciousness. This is a useful indication from the practical point of view, as it can be estimated at an interval after the injury from the duration of amnesia following the injury. This may be calculated by comparing the time of the injury with the time or date at which the patient again became fully orientated with regard to time and place. The duration of loss of full consciousness is estimated in this way in the following tables. In Table VI, this duration of loss of full consciousness is compared with the duration of incapacity. The cases in which a compensation factor is present are again included in separate columns. The increased liability to prolonged incapacity of the more severely injured patients is evident to some extent, but the most significant feature of this table is the high proportion of severely injured cases that were able to return to work within six months of the injury. This is all the more striking if we exclude the later age-periods from the analysis. Thus in Table VII all cases over the age of 40 years are excluded. In this group of working men and women, numbering 110 in all, only seven had not returned to full work eighteen months after the injury, and in three of these cases some compensation question was not yet settled. As will be seen from this table, most of the severe cases with prolonged loss of consciousness occurred in the younger age-periods, and it is a remarkable testimony to the power of recovery of the young adult that so many were able to resume full work, which in most cases involved hard manual labour.

The effect of the compensation factor is well seen in Table VI. There were 20 compensation cases in which the duration of loss of consciousness was less than one hour.

The mortality rate of the series is 8 per cent. but cases which died within twenty-four hours of admission are not included in the series.

TABLE VI.—*Showing comparison of the duration of incapacity for full work with the severity of the injury as indicated by the duration of loss of full consciousness. Compensation cases are shown separately in columns marked "C"*

Period off full work	Duration of loss of full consciousness							
	0–1 hour		1–24 hours		24–72 hours		Over 72 hours	
		C		C		C		C
0 to 2 months	32	5	27	3	2	0	4	0
2 to 6 months	5	6	6	2	3	0	14	1
6 to 18 months	2	2	3	0	0	0	3	0
Over 18 months	2	7	3	1	0	0	6	0
	41	20	39	6	5	0	27	1
Totals (139 cases)	61		45		5		28	

TABLE VII.—*This table is similar to Table VI, but all cases over the age of 40 are excluded*

Period off full work	Duration of loss of full consciousness							
	0–1 hour		1–24 hours		24–72 hours		Over 72 hours	
		C		C		C		C
0 to 2 months	30	3	23	2	2	0	4	0
2 to 6 months	1	6	5	2	3	0	13	1
6 to 18 months	1	1	3	0	0	0	3	0
Over 18 months	0	3	1	0	0	0	3	0
	32	13	32	4	5	0	23	1
Total (110 cases)	45		36		5		24	

In practice skilled observation of the patient from hour to hour is difficult to provide, so it is very fortunate that the retrospective assessment of the duration of the amnesic period after the injury is a remarkably good guide to the duration of loss of full consciousness.

This amnesic period is therefore conveniently referred to as the period of post-traumatic amnesia (P.T.A.), and its value was reassessed during the Second World War in paper 6 (1943) in collaboration with C. P. Symonds from which this extract is taken.

In the course of our work at a military hospital for head injuries we have had to deal with two groups of cases—gunshot or bomb wounds, and a variety of head injuries due to accidents of a kind which may also occur in civil life. It is with this latter group that the present paper is concerned. There is much uncertainty among surgeons and physicians regarding the prognosis in these cases, as is shown by the great variety of opinion expressed on the optimum duration of rest in bed, the period of convalescence required, and the likelihood of return to useful duty in the Services. With the aid of a grant from the Medical Research Council we have been able to collect data which have a bearing on these problems, and at the suggestion of the council's committee on brain injuries we present a summary of our experience and conclusions.

Cases of accidental head injury admitted to this hospital may be divided into two groups. (1) Chronic cases which have been previously treated in other hospitals; many of these have been transferred because their progress, judged by expectation, has been unsatisfactory, and they therefore form a highly selected group. (2) Acute cases; a relatively unselected group, being usually admitted because the accident happened in the neighbourhood of the hospital, though many had been first admitted to a general hospital and subsequently transferred. Cases admitted to this hospital within 3 weeks of the injury have been included in the acute group. The series is thus not entirely representative of accidental injuries, such as would be seen in a large general hospital in an industrial area, because it does not include those cases in which the severity of the head injury, or associated injuries of other parts, forbade transfer within the period specified. Doubtless this explains why the number of deaths in our series was small.

The analysis covers 242 consecutive acute cases; 5 died, and 22 (9%) of the survivors were invalided out of the Service from this hospital. The remainder, 215 (89%), were returned to duty, and it is with the subsequent fate of this group that we are first concerned.

Post-traumatic amnesia in acute cases

One of us has previously emphasized that a convenient means of classifying the severity of head injuries is the duration of the post-traumatic amnesia (Russell 1932). This method is incomplete, because it takes no account of local injury to the skull, brain or cranial nerves, but it is useful provided these limitations are clearly recognized. Post-traumatic amnesia is taken to end at the time from which the patient can give a clear and consecutive account of what was happening around him. This can be estimated by careful questioning after recovery of full consciousness and normal orientation. Care is necessary to avoid two sources of error. One arises from accepting the patient's first memory of his surroundings as the end-point, when it has in fact been followed by a further period of clouded consciousness and amnesia. Such "islands" of memory are not uncommon and may be followed by further amnesia for a day or two; it is therefore the beginning of continuous memory which we prefer as our measurement. The second, though less common, error is to assume that because a patient is aware of what is happening around him he will be able to recall this later. This may lead to underestimation of the duration of the post-traumatic amnesia in a patient who is under observation in the acute stage of his symptoms. It is therefore necessary in cases of this type to check the duration of the amnesia some time after the apparent recovery of full consciousness, for example, before the patient is discharged from hospital.

In Table I the prognosis in those who survived is compared with the duration of the post-traumatic amnesia (P.T.A.). Of the 215 cases returned to duty, 193 (90%) have been followed up, and the table gives not only the number of those invalided from the Services in this hospital but also of those known to have relapsed and been invalided later. The figures show that as the duration of the PTA lengthens the prognosis becomes worse. There is a rise in the proportion of those invalided when the P.T.A. exceeds 1 day, and a further significant rise in the over 7 days group. But a third of the most severe cases (P.T.A. over 7 days) returned to duty successfully, and at the other end of the scale, of those with a P.T.A. of less than 1 hour (including

TABLE I.—*Surviving acute cases: Prognosis in relation to severity of injury*

Duration of P.T.A.	Cases	Invalided in hospital	Invalided later	Total invalided	No follow-up
Nil . . .	28	1 (4%)	2 (7%)	3 (11%)	1
Under 1 hour .	75	2 (3%)	6 (8%)	8 (11%)	9
1–24 hours	65	3 (5%)	5 (8%)	8 (12%)	7
1–7 days .	34	5 (15%)	3 (9%)	8 (24%)	2
Over 7 days .	35	11 (31%)	10 (29%)	21 (60%)	3
Total . .	237	22 (9%)	26 (11%)	48 (20%)	22 (9%)

Percentages are of the number in each subgroup

those with no amnesia), 11% were invalided. This table, therefore, indicates both the value and the limitations of the duration of the P.T.A. as a criterion of prognosis. All that can be said for it is that it is the best single criterion at present available.

A record of the type of duty performed was included in the follow-up questionnaire, and the proportion of those on duty who were reported to be on full duty, efficiently performed, was 82%. This did not, however, always indicate that the patient was still in the same medical category as before the accident.

TABLE II.—*Duration of treatment in acute cases with a satisfactory follow-up report after return to duty*

Months from injury to discharge to duty	Duration of PTA					
	Nil	Under 1 hour	1–24 hours	1–7 days	Over 7 days	Total
Under ½ . .	4 (4)	4 (3)				8 (7)
Over ½ . .	7 (7)	20 (20)	10 (10)	1 (1)		38 (38)
1–2 . . .	7 (6)	19 (19)	23 (19)	15 (12)	1 (0)	65 (56)
2–3 . . .	6 (5)	13 (10)	12 (5)	5 (3)	7 (4)	43 (28)
3–4 . . .		2 (0)	3 (2)	1 (1)	1 (0)	7 (3)
4–5 . . .				2 (1)	1 (1)	5 (4)
5–6 . . .					1 (1)	1 (1)
Over 6 . .						
Total . .	24 (22)	58 (52)	50 (39)	24 (18)	11 (6)	167 (137)

Figures in parentheses show patients doing full duty efficiently.
Duration of treatment (including rehabilitation) was less than 3 months in 154 cases (92%); of these, 129 were doing full duty efficiently.

Duration of hospital treatment and rehabilitation

The plan has been to continue with treatment in hospital, including graduated physical exercise, until the patient is ambulant and then to transfer him to a convalescent hospital nearby; there, supervised by the medical officer who had charge of him in hospital, he is given physical training of progressive severity, and mental occupation, until he is judged fit for return to duty.

Of 193 cases discharged to duty and successfully followed up, 167 were reported on duty. Table II gives the actual duration of treatment and rehabilitation of those who returned to duty successfully: 92% were treated for less than 3 months, and of these, 84% were reported by the medical officer of the unit to be doing full duty efficiently. On the other hand, 26 patients were returned to duty, but on the follow-up were found to have relapsed later; of these only 17 (65%) were under treatment for less than 3 months. The incidence therefore of relapse was not higher among those who had been treated for relatively short periods, from which it may be concluded that a relatively short period of treatment under conditions obtaining at this hospital, was not a factor of importance in causing relapse.

Comment

This study was of particular value in that it demonstrated a practical time-table for thorough rehabilitation after head injury at a time when the old ideas of prolonged physical rest were only recently being discarded. It demonstrated further that even in severely injured patients a vigorous programme of physical training was usually entirely satisfactory. Nevertheless the proportion of those injured who failed to recover fitness for duty rose steeply in relation to a longer P.T.A.

In these studies special attention has been given to fitness for full physical activity, but of course this is not always the best criterion for recovery. Thus in the case of high-grade brain workers the criteria for recovery are more the return of full intellectual capacity and endurance, powers of concentration, and ability to learn new material. These last aspects of recovery and their relation to P.T.A. and to age have probably not yet been studied in the detail necessary.

The traumatic amnesias were assessed more fully in paper 7 (Russell and Nathan 1946, extract from pp. 281–6).

The duration of post-traumatic amnesia (P.T.A.) can only be estimated with accuracy after the patient has recovered from even slight degrees of confusion. This duration of P.T.A. will then usually remain relatively constant and will form a permanent index of the duration, not of unconsciousness, but of impaired consciousness. The P.T.A. therefore provides a useful clinical guide for the physician who may enquire into the case for the first time long after the injury occurred. It is obvious that the duration of P.T.A. will provide some indication of the severity of the general brain commotion caused by the injury, and studies by Symonds and Russell (1943) indicated its usefulness in prognosis. We have again analysed these Service cases with reference to subsequent fitness for *full duty* in a series followed up successfully through the Unit medical officers. The results are given in Table I and indicate clearly that the prospects of good recovery of efficiency diminish rapidly as the P.T.A. lengthens.

TABLE I.—FOLLOW-UP—*Duration of Post-Traumatic Amnesia compared with future fitness for full duty—based on follow-up of surviving cases six to twenty-four months after discharge from hospital. Cases were those admitted in the acute stage and therefore relatively unselected. Only those followed-up successfully are considered*

Duration of P.T.A.	*Total cases admitted to hospital*	*Ret. to duty from hospital*	*"Fully duty efficiently" on follow-up*	*Per cent of total*
Nil	29	28	25	86%
1 hour	92	90	80	87%
1–24 hours	73	70	54	74%
1–7 days	39	34	23	59%
7 days	41	26	7	17%
No record	2	2	1	
	276	250	190	69%

Duration of P.T.A.—This analysis in Table I is concerned with accidental blunt injuries in which the rate of change of velocity to which the skull is subjected probably determines the degree of brain damage (Denny-Brown and Russell, 1941). In gunshot wounds, on the other hand, the brain is often submitted to little acceleration, and as in other penetrating injuries the damage is often quite local.

TABLE II.—*Duration of Post-Traumatic Amnesia in a consecutive series of surviving "accidental" and gunshot wound cases admitted to a Military Hospital for head injuries.*

		Duration of P.T.A.					
	Total	Nil	<1 hr	1–24 hr	1–7 days	7 days	No record
"Accidental" head injury	1,022	99	208	312	231	167	5
Per cent		10%	20%	31%	23%	16%	½%
Gunshot wounds of the brain	200	64	40	22	42	24	6
Per cent		32%	20%	11%	21%	12%	3%

Thus in Table II the duration of P.T.A. is compared in a series of accidental injuries and of gunshot wounds of the head with dural penetration or skull fracture. No less than 32 per cent. of the gunshot wound cases have no amnesia, and this must be due to a failure of many of these missiles (which include small bomb fragments) to concuss the brain as a whole. There is also a remarkably small proportion of cases of gunshot wound with P.T.A. of one to twenty-four hours. This is in striking contrast to the "accidental" group and indicates that when gunshot wounds do cause loss of consciousness the latter is likely to be either of very short or of much prolonged duration. This can probably be explained by the assumption that when such wounds are of sufficient severity to cause severe general commotion the associated brain destruction will ensure by its extent or its complications that the P.T.A. is prolonged.

Table III gives the number of cases in the various P.T.A. groups in an unselected series of acute hospital admissions. The cases were admitted to a Military Hospital for Head Injuries, and were those admitted in the acute stage only; they are compared with figures for general hospitals published by one of us (W. R. R.) and also by Gutmann. There is a close similarity between the figures in the first two groups of cases, while those in Gutmann's series have a larger proportion of slight injuries.

TABLE III.—*Duration of Post-Traumatic Amnesia in a series of surviving cases admitted to hospital in the acute stage and therefore relatively unselected.*

	Total	Duration of P.T.A.					
		nil	<1 hr	1–24 hr	1–7 days	>7 days	No record
Military Hospital cases . .	331	34	115	91	45	43	3
Per cent .		10%	35%	27%	14%	13%	1%
Russell's (1932) cases Edinburgh .	184	80		57	47		
Per cent .		43%		31%	25%		
Gutmann's (1943) cases Oxford .	179	118		39	19	3	
Per cent .		66%		22%	11%	2%	

It is now generally agreed (Symonds, 1932; Russell, 1932; Greenfield, 1938; Jefferson, 1942) that the disorders of consciousness following head injury are usually dependent on neuronal trauma and are rarely due to vascular complications such as haemorrhage, oedema or increased intracranial pressure. Study of the duration of amnesias following injury carries us a step further, for this makes it necessary to postulate many degrees of neuronal commotion which, for example, may recover fully in ten minutes or may "feel their way" gradually to recovery in ten days.

Reduction of P.T.A.—Though the duration of P.T.A. is usually more or less permanent and unchanging, there are exceptions. Occasionally it becomes reduced spontaneously as in the following case:

Fus. R. sustained a head injury on July 19, 1942. On August 4 he had a momentary retrograde amnesia (R.A.) and a P.T.A. of six days with an "island" on the fourth day. Ten weeks after the accident he regained spontaneously another island in the P.T.A., for while sitting quietly in bed he suddenly remembered being on the floor of a moving truck, and this was, in fact, the way he was brought to hospital.

Cases of reduction in P.T.A. under barbiturate hypnosis are described later. These recoveries of things forgotten are reminiscent of hysterical amnesia and yet there is no reason to suppose they are hysterical.

Delayed P.T.A. and lucid interval.—In some few cases of accidental head injury all details of the injury and of events which closely followed it are clearly recalled, but there follows later a period of confusion and amnesia. This can be referred to as *delayed post-traumatic amnesia*. In most cases, especially in gunshot wounds of the brain, the delayed P.T.A. probably indicates that vascular complications of the wound are responsible for the delayed amnesia. 2.5 per cent. of 1,029 cases of accidental head injury had delayed amnesia, while the figure for gunshot wounds of the skull and brain was much higher, being 14 per cent. in 372 cases. In a very few cases of relatively slight injury the short lucid interval seems to correspond with a period of intense stimulation for the patient which may "keep him awake" for a time. For example, a cyclist whose motor-cycle caught fire after the accident remembers trying to put out the fire and then no more for many hours. Or again an airman after a crash remembered turning off the petrol before his P.T.A. developed. In this type of case the disturbance of consciousness is relatively slight and a strong stimulus may lead to registration of an event so well that it can be subsequently recalled.

The phenomenon of a lucid interval has for long been recognized as a clinical feature in the diagnosis of extradural haemorrhage. It should be noted, however, that it is only those cases which have little initial concussion which show this well-developed lucid interval before cerebral compression supervenes. It is equally important to note that there may be a lucid interval followed by delayed confusion in the absence of any gross intracranial complication such as haemorrhage. This is usually easy to distinguish clinically from the progressive stupor and coma of cerebral compression. These slight degrees of delayed confusion appear sometimes to be due to subarachnoid haemorrhage, or to minute intracerebral haemorrhages in the brain-stem (Denny-Brown, 1941).

Islands of memory in P.T.A.—The loss of memory for all events during the time covered by the P.T.A. is not always uniformly complete. In some cases islands of memory emerge which are often concerned with special events such as an operation or the visit of a relative. They are liable to appear when confusion is slight and the patient able to converse and behave in a sensible way. In 13 cases showing an early island in the P.T.A. the final duration of amnesia was one to twenty-four hours in 4 cases, one to seven days in 4 cases, and over seven days in 5 cases. In most of these cases of early islands in the P.T.A. the underlying factors are probably the same as in the cases of delayed amnesia already referred to, but the injury being more severe there is immediate loss of consciousness, then partial recovery or lucid interval corresponding to the "island", and then the delayed amnesia due to vascular complications. As with cases of delayed amnesia, the "island" with subsequent deterioration does not usually indicate that a serious degree of cerebral compression is developing. These islands, when they occur, cannot be localized, for they concern an isolated happening unconnected with the normal chain of memories—restricted paramnesias as Bannister and Zangwill (1941) term them. A special occasion may sometimes appear to be responsible for the return of continuous remembering and the end of the P.T.A. The suddenness with which the patient may "come to himself" is often a striking feature, and is of interest in considering the physiology of P.T.A.

Behaviour during period of P.T.A.—During the stages of recovery of consciousness many remarkable abnormalities are observed. In the first place the patient's behaviour may closely approximate the normal, and many football players have continued the game and have even played well after a head injury, though they subsequently remember nothing of that part of the game which followed the concussion. Their behaviour may be such that their friends notice nothing amiss, but in other instances there is obvious confusion, as for example the football player who after a head injury plays towards the wrong goal.

Similar abnormalities are sometimes observed after epileptic fits, where again the patient's inability to recall his actions is a striking feature. The term *automatic behaviour* is used to describe this condition, but it must be stressed that the term may refer to behaviour which is obviously confused, or on the other hand to behaviour which is outwardly normal and rational, but in which only the loss of recall indicates that a high level of cerebral function is in abeyance.

Conversation during period of P.T.A.—Many interesting aphasic phenomena occur during recovery from concussion, but these will not be considered here. When the patient is still severely confused he may occasionally give information regarding his injury which is subsequently quite forgotten. Burton (1931) has found that this information may be correct, but care must be taken not to be misled by confabulation.

Case of Memory Regarding Accident During Period of Confusion which was Later Forgotten within R.A.: Confabulation and False Accusation.

W. D. (*Case* P 91), an electrician aged 38, had a motor-cycle accident on 8.8.33, while swerving to avoid a dog. There was a laceration in the left frontal region and a linear fracture of the middle fossa of the skull. Two days after the injury he repeatedly said "It was a dog!" He was however quite confused, and gave the date as February, 1933. He gradually became more alert and confabulated aggressively regarding this early memory, and some information probably derived later from his wife. On 16.8.33 he gave the date and place correctly and said he had been in hospital for a week. "I'm supposed to have had a smash up, but it wasn't my fault—dog flew at me and I flew at it—a big black dog with a white spot on its chest. Farmer's son turned on me and smashed me with an instrument in his hand for damaging him. He is getting arrested to-day—plain clothes officer told me he had been arrested—that is one of the charges I have against him. I've the money to fight the case. I can prove what I said . . . The police have found the instrument, and everything is turning out as I said. Marks on the instrument and everything . . . the dog did not harm me . . . it was the man that hurt me . . . etc."

The condition improved steadily and he was discharged home about three weeks after the accident and resumed work two months after leaving hospital. When re-examined on 9.1.34 he had no recollection of his period in hospital except the last four days (P.T.A. sixteen days). The R.A. was two days, and those two days were a "complete blank." He was quite fit with no headache or giddiness and he considered his work capacity and memory to be as good as ever.

A witness, who was near when the accident occurred, said it was due to his swerving to avoid a large, black dog with white spots belonging to the adjacent farm. The farmer's son accompanied the patient to hospital in the ambulance, but the patient has now no idea even what the farmer's son looks like.

Occasionally the P.T.A. lengthens in the early days after recovery of consciousness as though the memory of events soon after recovery of consciousness is not retained with sufficient firmness for recall at a much later date. Barbiturate hypnosis may facilitate recall as in the following case:

Case of Lengthening P.T.A. Subsequently Reduced by Barbiturate Hypnosis.

Spr. C. had a R.A. of a few seconds. When questioned *seven* hours after the accident his first memory was of being lifted on to a stretcher. From the account of a witness of the accident this was half an hour after it occurred. Then he remembered nothing more until he heard someone saying that he needed two stitches in his lip: this was half an hour later. When questioned again *one week* after the accident, his first memory of being lifted on to a stretcher had gone, and the earliest memory now was someone saying he needed two stitches. The memory of the entire day of the accident was then vague, whereas it had been quite clear at the first examination. A fortnight after the accident his remembrances were unchanged but his memory of the day of the accident had become even more vague, and he could not give a satisfactory account of his medical examination on the day of admission. Under pentothal, however, he remembered being lifted on to the stretcher, and he also remembered an old lady saying: "Lift him carefully; he's badly injured." (This remark was confirmed by the police.) He now remembered part of the journey in the ambulance, but thought he must have gone to sleep for the last part of it, as he remembered nothing more until he was being stitched. His memory of his medical examination on admission remained, however, as vague as before.

The value and limitations of P.T.A. as an index of severity were analysed in greater detail in paper 16 based on the same hospital records (Russell and Aaron Smith 1961, extract from pp. 5–17).

Description of the population: Clinical groups

The clinical material available was highly selected from several different aspects. Some of the patients had been admitted to the hospital within 3 days following injury. These patients suffered their injuries near the special hospital, and they constituted a relatively unselected group, providing data for the acute stage of injury (Group A). Other patients were admitted within 3 weeks of injury, either for the special rehabilitation facilities available or because of urgent complications requiring surgical intervention, special examinations, etc. The data for these cases reflect features of the subacute stage (Group B). These 2 groups of relatively unselected cases were submitted to a vigorous policy of rehabilitation in a relatively short time following injury. Thus, in Groups A and B, the proportions of cases with psychogenic symptoms were apparently reduced, owing to the successful efforts at rehabilitation and the relatively unselected nature of the population.

The largest group (Group C) consisted of 805 patients who had been transferred to the special hospital from other centers because of difficulties in either rehabilitation or assessment. The time of admission was over 3 weeks from date of injury. Thus, in addition to differences in selection, the data for these patients reflect features of the chronic stage.

The remainder of the population (Group D) consisted of patients also in the chronic stage, except that only cases with substantial neurological injuries and symptoms were carded. Thus, although patients in both Groups C and D in the chronic stage were more selected than those in the acute and subacute stages (Groups A and B), the basis of selection for all groups differed. The 4 groups which comprised the total population of 1,766 cases are:

Group	Stage	Admission to Oxford Hospital	No.
A	Acute	Within 3 days	266
B	Subacute	Within 3 weeks	239
C	Chronic	After 3 weeks	805
D	Chronic (selected)	After 3 weeks	456

The differentiation of the 1,766 cases into 4 different populations described above affords an opportunity to study possible differences among them as a function of their unique selection and character. Differences among these 4 populations also provide definition of the effects of temporal changes reflected in the different proportions of incidence in any given clinical feature and afford a broader base for comparisons of the results of the present study with those of other more or less similar populations.

Limitations on the use of P.T.A. as an index of severity

Certain types of injury may result in severe focal or diffuse damage without causing "acceleration concussion" in the sense in which the term was introduced by Denny-Brown and Russell (1941). Thus in a study comparing the different P.T.A. distributions of patients with penetrating gunshot wounds of the brain, shell wounds of the scalp and skull, and accidental closed head injury (Russell, 1951), almost half the patients with wounds caused by sharp objects or high-velocity missiles

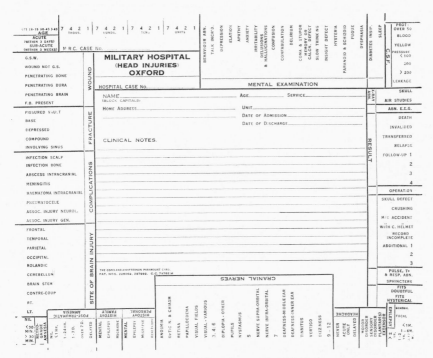

Card used for recording data on head injuries.

were either in the P.T.A.-nil category, or P.T.A.-less-than-1-hour category. In a second study of 15 cases with severe crushing injuries to the skull (Russell and Schiller, 1949), only 3 of the 15 patients suffered loss of consciousness. Since the severity of injuries in these patients was obvious, it is clear that in these types of injury, concussive effect is of secondary importance. Recognition of the limitations of P.T.A. thus provided a basis for screening the total population of the present study.

Therefore, in order to provide more homogeneous and comparable populations, similar cases in each of the 4 groups were analysed separately. The groups omitted from the data for the 4 populations presented below consisted of:

(1) Focal brain injury: Cases with depressed fractures, intracranial haemorrhage, abscess, or focal signs. In such cases, in addition to the secondary importance of concussive effects, the nature of the sequelae varies according to the specific site of the focal damage. In the present study, 146 cases of depressed fracture and 48 with

intracranial complications showed different distributions of P.T.A.'s. These cases were considered separately, and their P.T.A. distributions are presented in Table I.

(2) Cases with serious injuries to other parts of the body: In addition to head injuries, 238 patients of the total population also suffered severe injuries to other parts of the body. Although, as might be expected, the incidence of severe associated injuries increased with duration of P.T.A., any assessment of the effects of P.T.A. for disability, etc., would be confounded by the nature and severity of the associated injuries. The P.T.A. distributions for this group are also included in Table I.

TABLE I.—*P.T.A. Distributions for Exceptional Groups*

		nil		<1 hr		1–24 hr		1–7 days		>7 days	
	Total	No.	%	No.	%	No.	%	No.	%	No.	%
Depressed fractures	146	20	14	23	16	32	22	39	27	32	22
Intracranial complications	48	8	17	7	15	9	19	11	23	13	27
Associated injuries	238	12	5	48	20	49	21	60	25	69	29
Totals	432	40	9	78	18	90	21	110	25	114	26

The proportions of such cases among the 4 groups also define the character of the original populations: Group A, 30%; B, 30%; C, 18%; and D, 32%. Although the nature of their injuries makes them exceptional for analyses of effects restricted to P.T.A., their increasing incidence with longer P.T.A.'s also reflects the sensitivity of P.T.A. as an index of severity; ten cases for which data were incomplete were also excluded. The total number of cases remaining, 1,324 were distributed among Groups A, B, C, and D, respectively, as follows: 186, 168, 661, and 309.

Analysis of the data

All cases in each of the 4 groups were divided on the basis of an arbitrary 5 point scale for duration of P.T.A.: nil, less than 1 hour, 1 to 24 hours, 1 to 7 days, and over 7 days. After this, the incidence of each clinical feature was calculated for each P.T.A. period as a simple proportion, by dividing the total number of cases with a specific feature by the total number of cases in the P.T.A. interval. Thus, if there were 100 cases with P.T.A.'s over 7 days, and 50 of them had suffered a fractured skull, the incidence was 50% for this clinical feature. An actual example drawn from the results of the present study more concretely illustrates the basic statistical methods of analyses and comparisons of the present study. Of the 186 cases in Group A, 23 had P.T.A. nil; 75, less than 1 hour; 51, 1 to 24 hours; 13, 1 to 7 days; and 24 P.T.A.'s over 7 days. If we wish to study the effect of increasing P.T.A. intervals on invalidism, we then compare the proportion of patients in each P.T.A. interval who were invalided to the total number of cases in that interval. Thus, of the 23 in the P.T.A.-nil category, none (0%) were invalided; compared to 1 (1%) of the 75 in the P.T.A.-less-than-1-hour category, 2 (15%) of the 13 in the 1-to-7-days category, and 13 (54%) of the 24 in the P.T.A.-over-7-days category. The pattern of increasing incidence of invalidism with longer P.T.A.'s indicates that invalidism is one of the clinical features, the incidence of which is obviously affected by the duration of P.T.A.

Since, in analyses of a large number of variables in a single population, a pattern of increasing incidence would occur for some features purely as a function of chance, similar comparisons of the correlations between incidence and P.T.A. intervals for all 4 groups imposed a rigorous test of the sensitivity and reliability for any of the features found to be affected by P.T.A.

The results have been organized in terms of the fourfold purposes of the study. Some of the factors pertinent to the first purpose, definition of limitations of P.T.A. as an index of severity, have been described in the preceding section; other limitations are discussed in consideration of the results bearing on the remaining 3 purposes. Essentially, however, the relationship between incidence of clinical features and duration of P.T.A. is pertinent to all 4 factors. Accordingly, we have selected a representative sample of those clinical features the incidence of which systematically *increased* with longer P.T.A.'s in each of the 4 groups, and a sample of features the incidence of which was *unaffected* by the duration of P.T.A. in all 4 groups. Comparisons of the similarities and differences of the incidence of clinical features in the 4 groups thus provide evidence related to all 4 stated purposes.

Results

Table 2 presents the incidence of 10 different items included in the Figure. As all subjects in the 4 groups were service cases, some indication of the extent of disability is provided by the rate of invalidism (military discharges). The other 9 items consist of clinical features which have been divided into 2 groups. The first group consists of 6 signs or symptoms, the coincidence of which *consistently increased* with longer P.T.A.'s in all 4 groups, except for minor irregularities. These 6 positively correlated features were skull fracture, motor disorder, anosmia, dysphasia, memory and/or calculation defect, and retrograde amnesia over 30 minutes. The remaining 3 items consist of clinical features, the incidence of which showed a consistently *random* relationship to the duration of P.T.A. These noncorrelated features consisted of anxiety and depression, dizziness sans vertigo, and headache (never or acute only). (Since dull headache is a common symptom, the significance of this last feature in terms of severity is inversely proportional to its incidence, i.e., a high incidence of headache never or acute only, indicates a low proportion of dull headaches.)

In addition to the marked qualitative difference among the 6 signs and symptoms, the incidence of which *consistently increased* with longer P.T.A.'s, and the 3 in which the incidence was *unaffected* by duration of disturbed consciousness, the character of correlated and noncorrelated clinical features obviously differs. Because the first 6 included definite signs or symptoms, either directly reflecting or strongly suggestive of structural alterations in the brain, we have arbitrarily designated these as primarily "organic" features. Correspondingly, because the second 3 items consisted of reactions that are primarily psychological or emotional in character, these have been arbitrarily referred to as primarily "nonorganic" sequelae. Although the decision to discharge a patient from military service was based on physical and/or psychological disability, the proportions of cases invalided provides a general measure of the duration of P.T.A. as an index of severity.

Service Disposal

As all but a few of the total population were followed up for at least 2 years, the proportions of invalidism for the 4 groups in Table II represent the total number of such cases after 2 years. Comparisons of the percentages invalided in each of the 4 populations show a consistent pattern of increases as the duration of P.T.A. increases. Thus, despite the differences in selection factors and the influence of psychogenic factors, the consistent positive correlations are a striking illustration of the reliability and sensitivity of P.T.A. as an index of severity in these 4 different populations.

Although the pattern of increasing invalidism with longer P.T.A.'s was consistent for all 4 groups, comparisons of the *total* proportions invalided from each group range from a low of only 11% (for the acute unselected cases in Group A) to a high of 67% (for the chronic cases in Group C, with a high proportion of psychogenic factors). The most marked evidence of the differences among the 4 groups may be observed in comparisons of the proportions invalided in each of the 5 P.T.A. categories. Although the difference in total proportions of invalided cases for Group A (11%) and Group C (58%) is reflected in the P.T.A.-nil groups (Group A, 0% and Group C, 44%) comparisons of the cases with P.T.A. over 7 days show only a small difference between the percentages invalided (54% for Group A and 67% for Group C). Similar comparisons of all 4 groups show that the significance of P.T.A. as an index of severity changes with the character of the population.

An earlier study by Symonds and Russell (1943) of approximately 50% of these cases reported similar findings in comparisons of only 2 populations, acute and chronic. Although the proportions of cases with P.T.A. over 7 days were identical (60%) for acute and chronic cases, the percentages invalided in the shorter P.T.A. groups were much higher for chronic cases. Further study of the character of the 2 groups showed an incidence of 42% of family and/ or personal history of mental instability for the chronic cases, compared with only 17% for acute cases. The higher proportion of invalidism for low P.T.A. groups in chronic cases was thus attributed to a higher concentration of cases with a predisposition to psychological disability.

Although comparable data of family and/or personal history of mental instability are lacking for the 4 different groups of the present study, the availability of definitive data on duration of P.T.A. and comparisons of the incidence of primarily "organic" signs and symptoms and "nonorganic" sequelae, which are primarily psychological in character, afford an opportunity to define further the extent to which each of these features contributes to the incidence of invalidism. The results considered thus far clearly show that in an unselected population (the acute cases in Group A), correlations of P.T.A. and the crude measure of disability indicated by discharge from military service demonstrate that the duration of P.T.A. is a sensitive and reliable index of severity. As populations become more selective, however, although the rate of invalidism continues to rise with longer P.T.A.'s, the *nature* of the disability resulting in invalidism as well as the total proportions invalided changes as a function of non-organic factors that are unaffected by duration of P.T.A. As Symonds and Russell observed for their 2 populations, systematic differences in the concentrations of non-organic factors may also be noted as a result of the unique selection factors of the 4 groups in the present study. Comparisons of the proportions of each of the 6 "organic" and 3 "nonorganic" sequelae also provide further evidence of the significance of P.T.A. as an index of severity.

Incidence of Signs and Symptoms

Much has been written on the variety of psychogenically and organically determined symptoms following head injury that have been grouped into variously defined post-concussional syndromes. Although the correlation of P.T.A. and

TABLE II.—*Comparisons of Incidence of Invalidism and Selected Clinical Features with Increasing P.T.A. Intervals in the 4 Populations*

	Group	Total No.	%	nil No.	%	<1 hr No.	%	1–24 hr No.	%	1–7 days No.	%	>7 days No.	%
P.T.A.	A	186	—	23	12	75	40	51	27	13	7	24	13
	B	168	—	14	8	44	26	37	22	39	23	34	20
	C	661	—	59	9	117	8	224	34	156	24	105	16
	D	309	—	19	6	36	11	67	22	99	31	88	29
Invalided	A		11		0		1		9		15		54
	B		27		14		20		24		23		47
	C		58		44		53		58		60		67
	D		44		42		44		33		42		56
Primarily "Organic" Sequelae													
Fractured skull	A		25		9		13		25		54		67
	B		39		50		23		35		46		50
	C		20		3		10		14		31		35
	D		46		42		43		40		49		50
Anosmia	A		9		4		3		6		38		21
	B		11		7		2		11		15		18
	C		9		2		2		5		15		20
	D		18		5		6		9		24		27
Dysphasia	A		4		—		—		—		—		33
	B		3		—		—		—		—		15
	C		2		—		1		—		1		7
	D		4		5		6		—		2		9
RA > 30 min	A		12		—		3		10		23		50
	B		17		—		—		3		23		53
	C		12		—		—		5		17		38
	D		19		—		—		6		15		45
Memory and/or calculation defect	A		13		4		4		4		23		67
	B		26		—		7		21		31		62
	C		23		14		11		14		28		54
	D		29		5		11		9		34		52
Motor disorder	A		8		—		1		4		32		29
	B		10		—		2		—		13		29
	C		5		2		3		—		3		22
	D		11		16		6		—		6		25
Primarily "Non-organic" Reactions													
Anxiety and depression	A		9		13		1		14		8		21
	B		21		14		30		5		23		29
	C		56		58		62		58		59		37
	D		29		16		31		24		34		30
Dizziness sans vertigo	A		4		13		1		2		8		4
	B		10		7		11		16		8		5
	C		41		36		45		46		43		22
	D		13		—		11		13		18		11
Headache (never or acute only)	A		54		48		60		63		46		25
	B		42		36		41		51		41		38
	C		9		14		12		6		5		14
	D		20		21		25		21		17		22

invalidism was consistent for all 4 groups, the higher proportions of military discharges in Group C reflected the influence of the higher proportions of psychogenic features. As described earlier, Group C consisted of chronic cases who had been transferred because of difficulties in rehabilitation and/or assessment. Although this was a chronic group, the proportion of P.T.A.-nil cases was higher than that of Group B (subacute, relatively unselected cases) and Group D (chronic, selected cases); the proportion of long P.T.A.'s for Group C was also lower than that of Groups B and D.

Since Group C contributed half of the total population, the heterogeneous mixture of cases with a high proportion of psychogenic features might be expected to confound assessment of actual severity of injury. (Assessment of the severity of injury in service patients in terms of "invalidism" is somewhat analogous to the assessment of civil head injuries, in which "compensation" is an equal if not more confounding factor.) However, comparisons of the 10 items in Table 2 provide a striking illustration of the influence of the methods of selection which distinguished Group C patients from those in Groups A, B, and D. In fact, the mixture of organic and psychogenic symptoms in Group C not only imposed a rigorous test of the sensitivity of P.T.A. as an index of severity but also afforded an opportunity to study the interplay, overlap, and separation of symptoms that were organically determined and those that were psychogenic or of doubtful origin. Thus, in addition to their contribution to the proportions of invalidism, the incidence of each of the 9 other items for the 5 different P.T.A. intervals further defines the differences in selection of the 4 groups.

The incidence of "organic" sequelae—fractured skull, anosmia, dysphasia, retrograde amnesia over 30 minutes, memory and/or calculation defect and motor disorder—may be noted to increase with longer P.T.A.'s in all 4 groups. However, of all 4 groups, the one with highest incidence of invalidism, Group C, shows the lowest total incidence in all "organic" signs, except memory and/or calculation defect in which its incidence was the second lowest. Conversely, in the remaining 3 "nonorganic" symptoms—anxiety and depression, dizziness sans vertigo, and headache—the proportions of Group C were the highest. As we observed earlier, in contrast to the systematic increase in incidence with longer P.T.A.'s by the "organic" sequelae, the incidence of the 3 "nonorganic" sequelae was unaffected by the duration of P.T.A. in all 4 groups. When we compare the total incidence of invalidism with the incidence of "organic" and "nonorganic" sequelae for all 4 groups, a clear and consistent pattern emerges. In addition to the disabilities resulting from "organic" sequelae, the incidence of which systematically increased with duration of P.T.A., the differing rates of invalidism also reflect the varying incidence of "nonorganic" sequelae. The increase in total invalidism from acute to subacute to chronic groups (from 11% for the unselected acute cases of Group A, to 27% for the subacute cases in Group B, to 58% and 44% of the chronic cases in Groups C and D) thus reflects the different character of each of the 4 populations. These marked and systematic differences in the total proportion of cases invalided from each of the 4 groups, which are reflected in comparisons of the percentages invalided from the P.T.A.-nil groups of all 4 populations, vanish with similar comparisons of the relatively comparable proportions invalided from the P.T.A.-over-7-day groups.

The extent to which each of the "organic" and "nonorganic" sequelae contribute to disability in terms of invalidism may also be studied in comparisons of the incidence of each feature in Table II. Although the systematic increase in invalidism with longer P.T.A.'s is also shown by Group C, the effects of "nonorganic" factors are clearly shown in their consistently higher proportion of military discharges when all 4 groups are compared. The difference between the positive correlations of invalidism and "organic" sequelae with P.T.A., compared with the random distributions of "nonorganic" sequelae has important implications, which are considered in the following section.

The Effect of Age on P.T.A.

In the preceding sections, some of the limitations on the use of P.T.A. were cited in the exclusion of exceptional cases in the present study. Influences of the methods of selection on P.T.A. in the 4 different populations were also described in comparisons of the variable incidence of invalidism and individual clinical features in the

TABLE III.—*Correlations of P.T.A. and Age*

	Total No.	nil %	<1 hr %	1–24 hr %	1–7 days %	>7 days %
Group A (in Years)						
Under 25	143	9	40	31	7	13
26–35	93	13	40	22	10	16
36–45	24	4	29	25	17	25
Group B (in Years)						
Under 25	120	7	22	28	25	19
26–35	93	9	25	24	22	22
36–45	23	4	22	9	35	30
Group C (in Years)						
Under 25	399	10	15	31	28	17
26–35	314	9	22	30	21	18
36–45	79	11	16	28	24	20
Group D (in Years)						
Under 25	200	7	13	26	28	28
26–35	210	7	12	18	33	30
36–45	38	3	16	16	29	37

present study. However, one of the most important considerations in the assessment of effects of head injuries is age. In the first systematic studies of the significance of the duration of P.T.A., Russell wrote, "the age of the patient seems to be the most important single factor in estimating the prospect of recovery" (1934). The results of comprehensive analyses of effects of age in the 4 populations are in accord with Russell's earlier findings. Owing to the specific focus of the present paper, presentation of the results of analyses of effects of age has been restricted to only those findings illustrating its influence on P.T.A.

The 1,766 service cases afforded comparisons of 3 age groups: 18–25, 26–35, and 36–45 years old. Correlations of age with duration of P.T.A. are presented in Table III. Mr. Lewin, F.R.C.S., has kindly given us access to 1,000 consecutive records of acute civilian cases, permitting extension of age comparisons to groups from 6–15, 16–25, 26–35, 36–45, 46–65, and over 65 years old. To permit comparisons of Mr. Lewin's data (Table IV) with those of the present study, only cases with definite records of P.T.A. were included.

Comparisons of Tables III and IV clearly show that the incidence of long P.T.A.'s systematically increased with age in each of the 4 populations of the present study as well as in Mr. Lewin's population. The consistently higher proportions of long P.T.A.'s in our total population of acute, subacute, chronic, and chronic selected cases when compared with the acute consecutive cases provided by Mr. Lewin is further evidence of the previously cited influences of selection on P.T.A.

TABLE IV.—*Correlation of P.T.A. and Age in Mr. Lewin's Cases*

		Duration of P.T.A.				
Age (in Years)	No.	nil %	<1 hr %	1–24 hr %	1–7 days %	>7 days %
6–15	122	19	52	19	4	6
16–25	256	7	51	26	9	10
26–35	128	6	41	21	10	11
36–45	123	8	42	16	5	15
46–65	133	12	49	31	5	15
>65	62	16	50	32	7	17

TABLE V.—*Interactions of P.T.A. with Age*

	Duration of P.T.A.				
	nil %	<1 hr %	1–24 hr %	1–7 days %	>7 days %
Memory and Calculation Defect (in Years)					
Under 25	8	4	12	26	52
26–35	9	11	8	31	59
36–45	25	14	25	38	64
Fissured Fracture of Skull (in Years)					
Under 25	11	13	20	31	34
26–35	10	17	22	30	39
36–45	0	19	6	45	56
Motor Disorder (in Years)					
Under 25	3	6	1	6	25
26–35	8	7	2	9	27
36–45	17	0	17	12	35
Anosmia (in Years)					
Under 25	3	5	7	14	20
26–35	8	3	10	20	24
36–45	0	3	8	26	26

Since, apart from its significance as an index of severity, disturbed consciousness is a feature that is found in most cases of head injury, and the effects of cerebral trauma have been generally recognized to be more drastic in older patients, the increased incidence of longer P.T.A.'s in older subjects is hardly surprising. However, in addition to influencing the incidence of P.T.A., the age factor provides a further basis for evaluating the significance of the duration of P.T.A. By taking both age and duration of P.T.A. into account, or, in other words, the *interaction* of these 2 factors, the assessment of severity in closed head injury is considerably more reliable than when such assessment is based upon only 1 of the 2 factors. To illustrate this example of further definition of the significance of P.T.A., interactions between age and duration of P.T.A. on 4 clinical features in the total population are presented in Table V.

The pattern of increasing incidence with longer P.T.A.'s and advancing age is generally consistent for memory and/or calculation defect, fissured fracture of the skull, motor disorder, and anosmia. Thus, although the duration of P.T.A. is partly determined by age, the significance of the duration of P.T.A. as an index of severity is also partly determined by the age of the patient. As Table V shows, for patients with longer P.T.A.'s, the degree of severity may also be expected to vary with age, since the incidence of all 4 clinical features in Table V is higher for older subjects than for younger subjects. It is interesting to note that *all 4 symptoms the incidence of which systematically increased with longer P.T.A.'s also increased with advancing age*. Analysis of effects of age on anxiety and depression, dizziness sans vertigo, and headache (never or acute only), revealed that these symptoms, the incidence of which was not affected by P.T.A., were also *unaffected* by age. The striking consistency in the effects of duration of P.T.A. on one group of clinical features and the lack of effect on a second group of symptoms in all 4 populations, and a corresponding division of the same clinical features in terms of their sensitivity to age provided a basis for differentiation of the 2 groups of signs and symptoms.

Organic vs. Psychogenic Sequelae

Thus far, symptoms have been classified on a statistical basis. Table II reveals 2 groups of clinical features, the first showing a clear and consistent correlation of increasing incidence with longer P.T.A.'s, the second, random distributions with duration of P.T.A. The significance of the difference was further emphasized and defined by the fact that analysis for the effects of age resulted in an identical division.

When we compared the nature of the 2 groups of symptoms, the difference in their character was obvious. The first group, memory and/or calculation defect, skull fracture, anosmia, and motor disorder were representative of the fairly compelling signs of structural alteration of several features listed in Figure 1 (abnormal skull x-ray, air studies, E.E.G., epilepsy, plantars extensor, sensory disorder, etc.) that showed similar positive correlations but were excluded from this preliminary report for purposes of more economic and clearer exposition of the fourfold purposes. The second group was comprised of anxiety, depression, dizziness, and headache—all symptoms which are generally independent of structural changes. Since their incidence in Group C is as much as 8 times higher than that of the lowest group, the methods of selection unique to this group are obviously reflected in the results of analyses and comparison with other groups. The prominent difference in selection factors for Group C was inclusion of a high proportion of cases with psychogenic features, suggesting a further definition of the differences between the 2 groups of symptoms in terms of "organic" and "primarily psychogenic" features. The differentiation of signs and symptoms which are primarily or wholly organic in origin (i.e., those sequelae that are direct expressions of structural alterations, assumed or demonstrable) from those that are nonorganic (reactions sometimes referred to as "psychogenic," "functional," "hysterical," "neurotic," etc.) has obviously important implications, the practical and theoretical significance of which are elucidated below.

Comment

Nature of the Trauma.—Although much has been written of the common type of accidental head injury, the nature and magnitude of the distorting forces to which the brain is suddenly subjected may be appreciated by a simple example. If a patient has fallen on a hard surface, the velocity of the head striking the surface is V feet per second, and the distance through which that velocity is reduced to zero is S feet, then the acceleration, a feet per second^2 can be calculated by the formula

$$a = V^2/2S$$

Thus, where V is 30 ft/sec, and $S = \frac{1}{2}$ in. (or 0.04 ft.), then the acceleration is

$$\frac{900}{2 \times .04}$$

or 11,250 ft/sec^2 (350g). It is not surprising, therefore, that the forces associated with such sudden high accelerations should result in severe structural stresses and varieties of dislocations of brain structures described by Holbourn (1943) and elegantly photographed by Pudenz and Sheldon (1946).

The immediate observable effects of the physical injury to the complex organizations of neurons throughout the brain range from a momentary daze followed by recovery within a few minutes, to prolonged coma ending in death. As the data for the present study show, there is no loss of consciousness in only a small proportion of head injuries in the hospitalized cases of our series and varying intervals of P.T.A. for the overwhelming majority (over 90% in our total population). The degree and duration of suspended normal brain function is thus obviously an indication of the severity of effects of the distorting forces on the neurons of the brain, as the increasing proportions of sequelae associated with the duration of P.T.A. have demonstrated in the 4 highly variable populations.

Effects on Consciousness.—The importance of differentiating the various states of impaired alertness resulting from trauma was appreciated by Jackson (1874), who studied the effects of consciousness "from the slightest confusion of thought to deepest coma." In describing a case of concussion, he also distinguished between states following recovery from disturbed consciousness in terms of the patient's subjective experience. Head (1926) also differentiated the states following recovery from unconsciousness, calling attention to "that curious unwitting state during which he (the patient) is liable to act apparently reasonably but in a pure automatic manner." In his definition of a continuum for the different degrees of alertness, Head enunciated the concept of "vigilance," the normal state of "high grade physiological efficiency" of which normal conscious processes are an expression.

Thus, following trauma, the functions of the nervous system suffer reduced vigilance. Tissues of the nervous system, whether central or peripheral, brain or spinal cord or peripheral nerve—all show a capacity to recover function after a highly variable interval. Since consciousness is a function of the brain, there can be little doubt that the delay in recovery bears an important relationship to severity of injury in most cases. The restoration of full consciousness, in this sense, corresponds to Head's return of "vigilance."

As described in the original studies by Russell (1932, 1934), the length of the interval following trauma during which the patient was unable to store current events comprised the period of impaired consciousness. In addition to states of coma or unconsciousness, this period included "the curious unwitting state" described by Head, and is terminated at that point when, as Jackson described it, the patient reported that he "recovered his senses." Although some investigators have been reluctant to employ the patient's subjective report as a reliable datum, a distinct qualitative and obvious change in the patient's awareness and orientation is reflected by such questions as, "Where am I?"; "What am I doing here?"; or "What happened?" At this point, the events leading up to the accident may still be vague; however, from this point on, an important qualitative change in mental processes, restoration of the *capacity to store current events*, can be established by simple tests of recall. This operational definition of Jackson's term "recovery of senses" or Head's "vigilance" marks the end of the period of impaired consciousness. The question "What was the first memory after injury?" is thus an important one, and often permits a determination of the interval after the accident for which there is no memory of events in inquiries made long after the injury.

Limitations and Factors Influencing P.T.A.—As Brock (1960) has pointed out, in the absence of definitive evidence of structural damage, P.T.A. is the best "yard-stick" available. "Taken alone, this yardstick is not a perfect device, however." The results of the present study support both of Brock's conclusions. Of the approximately 100 different clinical features shown in the Figure, the duration of P.T.A. was by far the most reliable and sensitive index of severity. The results of the present study also provide further definition of factors influencing the sensitivity, reliability, and validity, as well as limitations in application of P.T.A. as a quantitative indicator of the extent of injury.

The bases for exclusion of exceptional cases define some of the limitations. As described above, fundamentally, the rationale underlying the use of P.T.A. as an index of severity in closed head injury is that the degree of generalized or diffuse cerebral disorganization following closed head injury is directly proportional to the duration of disturbed consciousness in most cases. However, in a small proportion of cases, the presence of focal signs or severe associated injuries limits the reliability of P.T.A. as a criterion of severity.

A further means of improving the P.T.A. "yardstick" is provided by results of the relationship between P.T.A. and age. In addition to the effects of age on duration of P.T.A., the significance of P.T.A. interval is further defined when the age of the patient is taken into account. Thus, assuming the same type and degree of head injury, older patients will tend to have longer P.T.A.'s, and, within any fixed P.T.A. interval, the severity of injury tends to increase with age.

Implications of the Results.—The most important results of the study which prompted preliminary presentation of a restricted but representative portion of the findings were the practical and theoretical implications of the use of P.T.A. as an index of severity. The gross differentiation of "organic" and "nonorganic" features is an instance of its methodological application. Among the organic sequelae, for example, the duration of retrograde amnesia, memory, and/or calculation defect, and confabulation have occasionally been considered to be psychogenic. Although there are undoubtedly instances of such cases, the consistent relationship of these clinical features to P.T.A. in all 4 populations, and especially in Group C, in which the proportion of psychogenic factors was high, remains clear and definite. Thus, in addition to its value as an index of severity, the capacity to discriminate the wide range of signs and symptoms in terms of their sensitivity to P.T.A. affords a criterion for classifying and evaluating post-traumatic sequelae.

In addition to the broad and arbitrary differentiation of "organic" and "non-organic" features, the significance of the individual symptom may be considered in terms of its incidence in a P.T.A. scale. Our total results show that certain symptoms occurred only rarely in P.T.A.'s of short duration. Whether such symptoms are reliable prognostic signs is a question for further study.

Classification of Head Injuries.—Another significant aspect of the results of the present study is the implications of the use of P.T.A. for prevailing diagnostic approaches to head injury. Current classifications of head injury, which arose in the days when little was known of the structure and function of neurons, are clearly incompatible with modern knowledge of the subject. Such classifications have traditionally depended on the probable naked-eye appearance of the brain should the patient die of the injury and a pathological examination be carried out.

There are, of course, certain surgical features or complications which require identification, such as a depressed fracture, a fractured base of skull, an intracranial hemorrhage, or an aerocele; but in most cases what is specially required is an indication of the severity and extent of brain cell damage.

The currently used criteria for indicating severity make use of terms such as cerebral "concussion," "contusion," and "laceration." None of these terms is, however, of much practical value in the classification of closed head injury, for by far the most important indication of severity is the effect of the injury on consciousness. Thus the occurrence of severe and prolonged coma—the worst type of closed head injury—has no satisfactory correlation with terms such as contusion or laceration, for the disastrous changes causing prolonged coma are often invisible to the naked eye (Strich, 1956).

It seems desirable, therefore, that the principal emphasis on the classification of head injuries should be on the effect on consciousness, both as regards the depth of unconsciousness and as regards the duration of disturbed consciousness. In this connection, the duration of deep coma is obviously important but difficult to assess without very frequent and expert examinations in the acute stage of the illness. In the absence of this information, the duration of P.T.A. comes to occupy a unique position in the classification of closed head injuries, as the present study clearly shows.

Concussion.—The term "concussion" has often been used to indicate a slight injury from which a complete recovery occurs, but this is really a meaningless category. On the other hand, the term concussion is expressive of neuronal trauma, and we would suggest that the classification *slight, moderate,* or *severe concussion* is an appropriate method of indicating the severity of neuronal damage in head injury.

Thus the terms could advantageously be used as follows:

Slight concussion: transient disturbance of consciousness; P.T.A. under 1 hour
Moderate concussion: as above, but P.T.A. 1 to 24 hours
Severe concussion: recovery of consciousness delayed; P.T.A. 1–7 days
Very severe concussion: prolonged coma or stupor; P.T.A. over 7 days

If there are surgical complications, the necessary qualifications may be added, as in the following examples: "moderate concussion with depressed fracture"; "slight concussion with extradural hemorrhage"; "severe concussion with fractured base of anterior fossa and aerocele."

These are suggestions from a variety of possibilities, but whatever method is adopted, the effect on consciousness and the duration of their effect provide the best criteria for classification at the present time.

Summary

The significance of post-traumatic amnesia (P.T.A.) as an index of severity was studied in 1,766 cases of closed head injury by correlating the incidence of clinical features with 5 different intervals of P.T.A.

Limitations of the application of P.T.A. were defined in the exclusion of exceptional cases from the total population.

Factors influencing the sensitivity and reliability of P.T.A. were demonstrated by division of the total remaining population into 4 groups on the basis of differences in selection.

Selected representative results, which showed systematic increases in incidence of most clinical features with longer P.T.A. in all 4 populations, also reflected population differences.

Analyses of the relationships of age and P.T.A. showed that the duration of P.T.A. increases with age and, that within fixed P.T.A. intervals, the incidence of clinical features rises with age.

Signs and symptoms that systematically increased with duration of P.T.A. showed the same relationship when correlated with age; clinical features that did not increase with duration of P.T.A. were also not influenced by age.

Signs and symptoms showing systematic positive correlations with increasing P.T.A. and age (which included signs of structural alterations) were arbitrarily defined as "primarily organic." Others that were unaffected by increasing P.T.A. and age (which were largely emotional in character) were arbitrarily defined as "nonorganic" or "psychogenic."

Of approximately 100 different signs and symptoms, P.T.A. emerged as the most sensitive and reliable index of severity for cases without signs of focal damage, such as depressed fracture or intracranial hemorrhage. The significance of the duration of P.T.A. is further defined by taking the age of the patient into account.

Practical and theoretical implications for prevailing diagnostic and classification methods of closed head injury and other applications of P.T.A. are discussed.

These papers therefore provide evidence that P.T.A. is a useful indication in retrospect of the severity of brain damage in closed head injuries. This finding can be correlated with the view that the basic commotion to the brain in these injuries is a physical distortion of a vast number of neurones, and that the duration of severely disordered function can be related to the severity of this physical effect. At a certain stage of severity the injury causes a proportion of cerebral axons to become torn across and the amount of this irreversible neuronal injury must also play a part in determining the duration of disturbed consciousness.

Strich (1956) demonstrated gross destruction of white matter in the cerebral hemispheres in some cases of traumatic dementia without there being the usual evidence of contusion or intracerebral haemorrhage. This evidently represents the consequences of gross distortional effects that in a minor form only cause a transient loss of full consciousness. This interpretation has received very strong support from the study by Oppenheimer (1968) in which he has demonstrated the widespread division of axons in the brain in head injuries of very minor degree. To quote from his paper (p. 306): 'The point to be stressed in regard to these cases of "concussion" is that permanent damage, in the form of microscopic destructive foci, can be inflicted on the brain by what are regarded as trivial head injuries.' Again, on p. 303, 'There can be little doubt that the lesions described here are of the same nature as those described by Strich in 1956 and 1961.'

It seems therefore that in all cases of closed head injury there is a mixture of distortion, shearing, and destruction of brain tissue, and that the relation of these factors to each other varies infinitely from case to case. This conception emphasizes the great difficulties of classification from the pathophysiological point of view, and yet this complicated picture makes more understandable the fact that the clinical state is often more accurately assessed by the duration of unconsciousness and later by P.T.A. than by any other means.

Many neuropathologists have reported degenerative changes in brain cells studied from fatal cases of head injury. The question naturally arises as to whether these changes are secondary to axonal division some distance away, and although this seems a likely explanation in most instances, the question has not yet been fully answered.

In paper 16, which has been reproduced in this chapter, some explanation is needed with regard to the so-called non-organic type of post-concussional symptom. It should, of course, be fully realized that symptoms such as headache, giddiness, depression, fatiguability, and anxiety may be direct or indirect results of neuronal injury or loss. The point is that these symptoms continue to be a serious source of complaint with some patients but not with others, and apparently without any relation to the severity or the physics of the injury. This variable state of affairs seems to depend on certain personal features of the individual. Nevertheless it is not usually correct to class such symptoms as being purely psychogenic in origin.

3

RETROGRADE AMNESIA

THE phenomenon of retrograde amnesia is one of the most significant of traumatic phenomena and its occurrence gives important information with regard to some aspects of brain physiology.

Some of the observations reported are as follows.

In paper 2 (Russell 1932, p. 565), recollection of the actual blow to the head was never subsequently remembered when immediate loss of consciousness had resulted from the injury. Thus:

After return of consciousness it was found in all cases that there was an interval immediately preceding the injury, of which the patient had no recollection. The duration of this interval, the period of *retrograde amnesia*, was inquired into carefully in ninety-six cases. In sixty-nine cases its duration was only one or two seconds, in twenty-four cases it lasted several minutes, while in only three cases was it of longer duration than half an hour. This interval was estimated by questioning the patient after full return of consciousness. If questioned before this, the interval of loss of memory before the accident was of considerably longer duration.

In the following table the duration of retrograde amnesia is compared to the groups into which the cases fall.

TABLE XI.—*Approximate Duration of Retrograde Amnesia*

Group	A few seconds	1 to 30 minutes	Over 30 minutes
A	35	4	0
B	29	8	1
C	6	12	2
	69	24	3

Group A unconscious for less than 1 hour
Group B unconscious for 1 to 24 hours
Group C unconscious for over 24 hours

The longer periods of retrograde amnesia are therefore more commonly found in cases which fall into Group C.

The recollection of events shortly preceding the accident may usually be taken as an indication that full consciousness has returned.

The duration of R.A. was studied in a larger series of cases in paper 7 (Russell and Nathan 1946, pp. 289–90).

The curious phenomenon of retrograde amnesia which is so well known in head injury is also found after electric convulsion therapy, status epilepticus, meningitis and acute cerebral anoxia as in hanging, CO poisoning and severe loss of blood. R.A. is for events which occurred before the injury while the patient was still fully conscious. The events occurring during this period were often dramatic and must have been registered by the normally acting sensorium, yet the injury intervenes and these events are thereby prevented from being retained, or if they are retained they cannot be recalled. The clinical features of R.A. present many interesting variations.

Duration of R.A.—The R.A. is in most cases for a few moments only. The motorist remembers approaching the cross-roads, the cyclist remembers losing control on a steep hill, or the window-cleaner remembers losing his balance. This momentary R.A. is observed after injuries of all degrees of severity and presumably has a clear and uniform physiological basis. In cases of prolonged R.A. other factors require consideration.

TABLE IV.—*Duration of P.T.A. and R.A. compared in 1,029 cases of "accidental" head injury (gunshot wounds excluded)*

| Duration of R.A. | Nil | Duration of P.T.A. | | | | | |
		<1 hr	1–24 hr	1–7 days	>7 days	No record	Total
Nil . . .	99	23	9	2	0	0	133
Under 30 minutes .	—	178	274	174	80	1	707
Over 30 minutes .	—	3	16	41	73	0	133
No record . .	—	4	14	14	15	9	56
Total . .	99	208	313	231	168	10	1,029

In Table IV the R.A. in 1,029 cases is roughly estimated, and compared with the P.T.A. In Table V, fifty consecutive cases from each P.T.A. group have the R.A. recorded in greater detail. These tables indicate how very constant some period of R.A. is in all injuries which disturb consciousness sufficiently to produce even a short P.T.A. These records were made by many observers, and some errors there

TABLE V.—*Detailed comparison of duration of P.T.A. and R.A. using 50 consecutive cases from each P.T.A. group*

| Duration of R.A. | Duration of P.T.A. | | | | |
	<1 hr	1–24 hr	1–7 days	>7 days	Total
Nil	9	1	1	—	11
1 minute . . .	34	35	15	12	96
1–30 minutes . .	6	13	21	18	58
1–30 minutes . .	6	13	21	18	58
½–12 hours . .	1	1	9	6	17
½–2 days . .	—	—	3	7	10
2–10 days . .	—	—	1	6	7
Over 10 days . .	—	—	—	1	1
Total . . .	50	50	50	50	200

must be. It is common, for example, in street accidents for the victim to remember being struck by a vehicle but nothing more. His head injury may, however, have been due to his striking the ground a second or two later, and this would be recorded according to our standards as a momentary R.A. Such cases may easily be entered in error as R.A.: nil. However, there is no doubt that certain cases of accidental concussion with a short P.T.A. clearly remember the head injury, and in Table V there are 11 cases of this type in 200 cases.

On p. 57 reference will be made to the traumatic amnesias that occur in relation to the very focal brain wounds caused by high-velocity missiles— the small metal fragments from the exploding shells and bombs of modern warfare. In many of these there is no amnesia at all, but in this group also, it is relatively common for the wound to be remembered although there follows an appreciable P.T.A. This occurrence is much more likely to occur in focal brain injury than in the typical acceleration concussion, so that when there is P.T.A. but no R.A. in the closed injuries, the injury is often of the missile type as in the following examples, quoted from paper 7 (Russell and Nathan 1946).

Case of Accidental Head Injury from a Falling Stone with R.A.: Nil, and P.T.A.: Twenty-four Hours

A quarryman (p. 6,203) was injured by a falling stone, which was about the size of a man's fist. The stone fell from a height of about 60 feet, and striking his head caused a fissure fracture of the skull in the parieto-occipital region. When questioned ten days after the injury he said that he remembered hearing the stone falling, and he ran to get out of the way. Then he remembers clearly a dull, crushing sensation in his ears, but nothing more until he came to himself in hospital twenty-four hours later. He did not remember falling to the ground after being struck. but the ground was soft, so that it is unlikely that he had a second injury while falling.

Accidental Head Injury: P.T.A.: One Hour, R.A.: Nil

A.M. (MRC 876) was playing goal in a football match. He remembers diving at the feet of the opposing centre forward, and deflecting the ball. He then remembers seeing a boot coming towards his face, then a blinding flash, but has no memory of the impact. He came to himself in hospital over an hour later.

This difference between acceleration concussion with its generalized cerebral commotion and a more focal type of cortical injury is not surprising, for the latter may inactivate a state of impaired consciousness more slowly by a spreading inhibition for a local area of the brain.

Comment

These reports indicate the general pattern of P.T.A. and R.A. which may be expected on questioning the subject long after the event and obviously form an important check on the validity of the record described. There are also, however, a number of variants and anomalies which are of particular physiological interest. The amnesias associated with missile wounds of the brain are considered later (p. 54).

Shrinkage of R.A.

One of the most remarkable features of the traumatic amnesias may be observed during the stages of recovery, as was reported in a later section (pp. 291–7) of the same paper.

During the gradual recovery of consciousness, while there is still some confusion, the R.A. is often very long. This may be so marked that the patient gives the date as several years previously with a corresponding reduction in his age. For example a Polish airman, who crashed in 1941, when questioned three weeks later, was still confused and said it was 1936, and when asked about war with Germany replied "We are not ready yet."

A case previously described (Russell, 1935) was that of P. A. S. (P 234), a greenkeeper, aged 22, who was thrown from his motor cycle in August, 1933. There was a bruise in the left frontal region and slight bleeding from the left ear, but no fracture was seen on X-ray examination. A week after the accident he was able to converse sensibly, and the nursing staff considered that he had fully recovered consciousness. When questioned, however, he said that the date was in February, 1922, and that he was a schoolboy. He had no recollection of five years spent in Australia, and two years in this country working on a golf course. Two weeks after the injury he remembered the five years spent in Australia, and remembered returning to this country; the past two years were, however, a complete blank as far as his memory was concerned. Three weeks after the injury he returned to the village where he had been working for two years. Everything looked strange, and he had no recollection of ever having been there before. He lost his way on more than one occasion. Still feeling a stranger to the district he returned to work; he was able to do his work satisfactorily, but had difficulty in remembering what he had actually done during the day. About ten weeks after the accident the events of the past two years were gradually recollected and finally he was able to remember everything up to within a few minutes of the accident.

R.A. at First for Six Months—Shrinking to a Few Minutes
P.T.A. Two Months

(MRC 516) was injured in an air-raid on 28.11.40. When first seen he was deeply comatose with flaccid limbs. Recovery of consciousness was very slow, and he did not begin to talk until a month later. On 11.3.41 his mental state was still greatly retarded. The R.A. was for about six months, and he had no recollection of three months in the Army. He now remembered coming to himself in hospital in January, 1941, when he found two women and a man sitting at his bed. These people told him they were his wife, mother and a close friend. He remembers arguing with them and saying he was not even married, and that he was certain he had never seen the man before. He was now correctly orientated, but was still very uncertain of the main facts concerning himself. He did all intelligence tests badly, and had difficulty in reading. He was very cheerful and friendly.

By 16.4.41, the R.A. had shrunk to a few minutes, and he remembers standing by the guns on the night he was injured, and that a few shells had been fired, but he does not remember any bombs; the P.T.A. was for about two months. He remained popular with the patients, but childish and slow in his movements with periods of irritability. He was invalided in May, 1941, and returned to light manual work in February, 1942. He found his right leg and arm "untrustworthy," and his relatives said he was forgetful and hesitated in his speech.

In one of this group of cases in which the patient, while still slightly confused but orientated, had a dense R.A. of about a year's duration, amytal was given in an attempt to recover the amnesia but without any improvement.

In these cases of slow shrinking R.A., the P.T.A. terminates long before the R.A. shrinks to its final duration. While the R.A. extends over many months or years the patient may, to careful testing, be slightly confused, but he has often recovered sufficiently to have continuous memory and to behave in a rational way.

During this period of shrinking amnesia the patient is unable to recall an important group of memories which, as later recovery shows, were well registered. The recovery occurs not in order of importance but in order of time. Long-past memories are the first to return, and the temporary blocking of relatively recent memory may be so marked that several years of recent life may be entirely eliminated. For a limited time the patient may re-live his childhood, a state of affairs reminiscent of the case of senile dementia.

During recovery the R.A. shrinks at a varying rate to a point where memory of subsequent events ceases abruptly. This usually leaves the duration of R.A. clearly indicated, but this can only be estimated accurately after full recovery of consciousness.

By the time the R.A. has shrunk to a few minutes or less the patient has usually fully recovered consciousness, and indeed a brief R.A. is often an accurate indication of mental normality.

Table V shows the increasing proportion of cases with a permanent long R.A. as the P.T.A. lengthens, though as has been mentioned the R.A. may be very short in severe injuries. In some cases this matter can be explained very simply, for in attempting to estimate the R.A. the patient who has emerged from a long P.T.A. endeavours to remember events which occurred perhaps over a week previously. Many uninjured individuals are unable to describe what happened a week ago, unless there is some special experience to remind them.

Prolonged R.A.—This simple explanation does not, however, explain the long R.A. in many cases, especially those in which events of importance to the individual were forgotten. It has already been suggested that the common momentary R.A. is due to a physiological effect of the injury which blocks the retention of events seen or heard in the moments before the concussion. Some very different explanation is required for the relatively long R.A. which may be recorded in severe cases with a long P.T.A. In Table V, 14 per cent. of the cases with P.T.A. over seven days reported R.A. of over two days. These periods of R.A. are completely blank to the patient and often cover important events.

An example of important memories lost during an R.A. lasting several days is the following case kindly provided by Sir Charles Symonds:

A flight-lieutenant, aged 31, was seen on February 7, 1936. Following a head injury when flying in 1934 he had been posted to ground duties which he had performed inefficiently, and was charged with being unable to account for stores to the value of £100. On examination he was orientated, voluble, facile and dysarthric. He could not retain more than six digits, showed three errors in repeating name, address and flower after five minutes, and failed in simple mental arithmetic. His face was expressionless with weakness of the left facial muscles. There were no other abnormal physical signs.

The head injury occurred in a crash on April 15, 1934, and there was a P.T.A. of twenty-one days. He came to himself in an eight-bedded ward which he describes in considerable detail, and has a consecutive memory of subsequent events. The story of his R.A. is as follows: The injury occurred on a Monday, and he had joined his unit eight days previously on a Sunday. He remembers arriving on the Sunday night and noticing that his room was of a different type from any he had slept in before. He has an isolated memory of firing at a ground target the following day, and of visiting a café sometime on that day

4

but has no recollection of the subsequent week. During this period he was on flying exercises of a kind he had not done before in an aircraft to which he was accustomed, doing several trips a day. He had studied his log book giving the details of these exercises over and over again in a fruitless attempt to recall the memory of these days. On May 21, 1927, he had had a head injury with a permanent R.A. of fifteen minutes and P.T.A. for three days followed by a headache for several days.

Islands in R.A.—It is clear that severe head injury may have a specific effect on very recently acquired memories, and this will be discussed later. A long R.A. with a P.T.A. of only twenty-four hours is very unusual, but the following case illustrates this:—

Case of R.A. with Islands for Over 24 Hours. P.T.A. 24 Hours. Investigation of R.A. Under Amytal Hypnosis Made Little Alteration.

A corporal (MRC 2039) was thrown from his horse on 20.7.41. He came to himself twenty-four hours later, and his memory thereafter is quite clear. When examined on 22.8.41 his memory of events before the injury was normal up to the morning of the day before the injury (19.7.41). On this day, over twenty-four hours before the injury, he remembers reporting sick at about 9 a.m. with synovitis of the knee. He was excused duties, but remembers little more of that day—he does not even remember leaving the M.I. room. His wife came to meet him that evening, but he has no memory at all of her visit except that he remembers getting into a bus with her, to see her home, and later being at a station near where she was staying. For the day on which the accident occurred he has no memory except one island—he remembers tying up his horse at the gate where his wife was staying, going to the house and being told his wife was out. From 9 a.m. of the previous day, therefore, there was complete amnesia, except for three short islands. When he came to himself on 21.7.41 his first memory was of tying the horse to the gate.

Under the influence of sodium amytal he became sleepy, euphoric and talkative. Repeated attempts were made to reduce the R.A. and P.T.A. or to increase the islands in the R.A., but without success, except that one further island appeared—he now remembered leaving camp on the evening of 19.7.41, and walking with his friend, Bill, past some sentries.

He made a good recovery, and went to a Convalescent Depot on 2.10.41. Eighteen months later he was Category A, and was then serving efficiently in the Middle East.

In most cases of persistently long R.A. the P.T.A. has also been long. The following are typical examples:—

A flying officer (MRC 2) crashed on 13.11.39. He was demonstrating a low attack on troops which he had done twice, but on the third attack he hit a tree and his crew of one was killed.

When examined in March, 1940, the P.T.A. was for twenty-eight days. His last memory before the injury was meeting an officer on the way to Ipswich, where the flying was to be. This was two days before the injury, and he has no memory at all of what happened during these two days before the crash.

He made a remarkably good recovery, returned to duty in an administrative capacity, and resumed flying duties successfully in January, 1942. He reported that he was very fit in January, 1944.

A junior officer (MRC 357) had a severe motor-cycle accident on 25.9.40. When examined on 23.11.40 the P.T.A. was complete for five days. About a week before the injury he remembers his unit taking up positions on the coast, and this was of course an exciting time with the prospect of invasion. However, his memory of the week before the injury is very vague. He has an indistinct memory of a demonstration and of one day's training a few days before the injury but otherwise his R.A. is dense for one week.

The injury caused some permanent intellectual impairment and personality disorder. He returned to duty, but found himself to be slow and easily muddled. There was permanent anosmia. He was, however, still in the Army in April, 1944, and his general health was satisfactory.

In these cases there is clear inability to recall important events which must previously have been well registered, retained and recalled before the injury. This type of amnesia is obviously different from the R.A. for events occurring a few moments only before an injury. When important events are obliterated from memory after head injury they are usually for relatively recent happenings. Recent memories are therefore more vulnerable than those that are remote, but it is remarkable that recent memories for important events should be so completely obliterated from memory as they often are. This long R.A. differs from the memory disorders of organic dementias. In both conditions recent memories are lost, but in the traumatic cases the ability to recall events since the injury has recovered well.

In the case of permanent long R.A. the memory loss resembles that which, as has been mentioned, is often observed during recovery from traumatic confusion, before the R.A. has shrunk down to its final length. In both types of case the relative vulnerability of recent memory is very evident. The retention of recent memories is evidently less firmly established and may, as in these last cases, be abolished permanently by the physical effects on the cerebral neurones of a severe head injury.

Association of ideas may assist the reduction of R.A., as in the case of a soldier who, after recovering consciousness, had an R.A. of over an hour—his last memory was setting out on his journey driving a truck in the dark. Some months later at the cinema he was watching the picture of an aeroplane crashing with the appropriate sounds. The patient found this a very upsetting experience, and suddenly the noise brought back to his mind the noise he heard as his truck crashed.

This type of case bears a remarkable resemblance to the behaviour of a repressed complex, in that an experience which had been registered and retained was not recalled except through an association of ideas, and this experience caused an emotional response which was appropriate to the forgotten material.

Effect of Barbiturate Hypnosis on R.A. and P.T.A.

It is obviously important that the possibility of altering the duration of traumatic amnesia under barbiturate hypnosis should be fully investigated, not only to preclude an hysterical factor in certain cases, but to investigate the possibility of using this method to reduce a purely organic amnesia. One of us (P. N.) has investigated 40 cases recovering from head injury under barbiturate hypnosis.

Method

On admission to hospital the patient's history was taken in the usual way, but special attention was paid to memory of events preceding, during and following the amnesic period. Within the next few days the patient was again interviewed, encouraged to relax and to attempt to describe all events preceding and following the injury. He was then given slowly an intravenous injection of sodium pentothal during a period of two to three minutes, until having passed through the stage of yawning he was no longer able to react to commands nor could respond to being shaken (the maximum quantity given was 0.5 grammes). He was gradually encouraged to waken by calling his name or being ordered to rouse himself. Having recovered consciousness sufficiently he was repeatedly pressed to recount all he knew of his accident and of the incidents which preceded and followed it. This was continued until he was able to walk back to bed unaided. During the following days or weeks he would be questioned again from time to time. Where possible the evidence was obtained from witnesses in order to check events elicited from the patient.

Results

From the investigation of 40 cases with barbiturate hypnosis it was quite evident that in the majority no reduction of amnesia could be obtained. Thus in 28 of the 40 cases investigated the R.A. and P.T.A. remained unchanged.

In the remaining 12 cases, however, some additional memory was recovered, though this was sometimes insignificant.

In 3 cases both the R.A. and P.T.A. were reduced.

L/Cpl. S. R.A. reduced from a few seconds to a moment.
P.T.A. reduced from five hours to one hour.
(Hypnosis two months after injury.)

Cpl. B. R.A. reduced from two hours to a moment.
P.T.A. reduced from eighty-six hours to seventy hours.
(Hypnosis seven weeks after injury.)

In 3 cases the R.A. only was reduced while the P.T.A. was unaffected.

L/Cpl. L. R.A. reduced from half an hour to nil.
P.T.A. reduced from forty-eight hours to nil.
(Hypnosis four weeks after injury.)

Cpl. S. R.A. reduced from sixty-five minutes to three minutes.
P.T.A. fifty-two hours—unchanged.
(Hypnosis five weeks after injury.)

Sgt. B. R.A. reduced from twenty minutes to a moment.
P.T.A. ninety-six hours—unchanged except for an island recovered in the partial amnesic period.
(Hypnosis five weeks after injury.)

Sgt. J. R.A. reduced from seven hours to half an hour.
P.T.A. sixteen hours—no change.
(Hypnosis four weeks after injury.)

In 2 cases the P.T.A. was reduced while the R.A. showed no change.

Dvr. E. R.A. half an hour—unchanged.
P.T.A. two days reduced by a few minutes only.
(Hypnosis three weeks after injury.)

In 4 cases the R.A. and P.T.A. were unchanged, but islands of memory during the amnesic period were recovered.

Spr. C. R.A. momentary—unchanged.
P.T.A. one hour reduced to half an hour.
(Hypnosis six weeks after injury.)

Cadet P. R.A. a few seconds—unchanged.
P.T.A. forty-eight hours—unchanged, but two brief islands of memory recovered.
(Hypnosis three weeks after injury.)

Gdm. McN. R.A. about five seconds—unchanged.
           P.T.A. fourteen days—unchanged, but several vague and brief islands of
           memory recovered.
           (Hypnosis three months after injury.)

Fus. K.   R.A. seven minutes—unchanged.
           P.T.A. three weeks—unchanged, but a few islands of memory recovered.
           (Hypnosis six weeks after injury.)

Dvr. S.   R.A. twelve hours—unchanged.
           P.T.A. eleven days—unchanged, but a few islands of memory recovered
           for the latter part of the amnesic period.
           (Hypnosis six weeks after injury.)

Analysis of the material recovered under pentothal showed nothing in this
material to warrant hysterical repression, and indeed the constancy with which the
recovered material borders the fringes of the amnesic period makes it seem probable
that the memories recovered were only incompletely abolished. They were recorded,
but could not be recalled without a special stimulus applied by questioning during
hypnosis. The examiner naturally stimulates the association of ideas, and the
spontaneous recovery of forgotten items by a later experience has already been
described.

These investigations under barbiturate hypnosis therefore provide confirmation
of the view that both the R.A. and P.T.A. in most cases is the result of physical
effect of injury on brain neurones.

Hysterical R.A.—Cases are described from time to time in fiction in which there
is a permanent R.A. for a large part of the whole of previous life. This may be
observed during the stages of recovery before confusion is fully resolved, but we
have never observed an R.A. to extend over many months permanently except in
hysteria or gross traumatic dementia.

Comment

The various phenomena that may be observed in relation to retrograde
amnesia provide some important clues with regard to the physiology of
memory, learning, and recall. As man is particularly orientated to the visual
aspects of experience it is inevitable that visual memories may be the easiest
to study. The various phenomena described are discussed later with reference
to the physiology of remembering.

OTHER PHENOMENA RELATED TO RETROGRADE AMNESIA

SOME curious phenomena in relation to the traumatic amnesias were referred to earlier in paper 4 (Russell 1935).

False Accusations

Another point in the study of cases recovering from concussion is that events which occurred immediately before the injury are occasionally remembered indistinctly during the period of confusion, even though there will be complete amnesia for these events after consciousness has returned in full. This memory may result in the patient making false accusations, as in the following case.

An electrical engineer, aged 38, while riding a motor cycle, swerved suddenly to avoid a dog which ran in front of him. He was brought to hospital on August 8th, 1933, in a stuporose state, and was found to have a fracture of the middle fossa of the skull. There was gross bruising in the left frontal region. When re-examined five months after the accident he reported that he was quite fit and had been working regularly for three months. He said that he had no recollection of events for a period lasting from two days before the accident to two weeks after it. There was not the slightest recollection of the accident itself.

When, however, this patient was examined two days after the accident, he was often heard to say, "It was a dog." Six days after the accident he was in a confused but very aggressive state and said: "I am supposed to have had a smash, but it wasn't my fault. A dog flew at me and I flew at it. The farmer's son turned on me and smashed with an instrument in his hand. He is getting arrested to-day. The police have found the instrument; everything is turning out as I said, marks on the instrument and everything." The accident was witnessed by several people, and the only connexion the farmer's son had with the accident was that he accompanied the patient to hospital in an ambulance.

This case is similar to one recorded by Somerville in which a doctor motored home a boy who had fallen off his cycle, and was subsequently accused by the boy of having run him down.

Burton (1931) studied the patient's conversation during the period of post-traumatic confusion and found that he may occasionally give information about his injury which is subsequently quite forgotten. Care must be taken not to be misled by confabulation, as appeared in the above examples of false accusation.

'Visions' related to the injury

Patients sometimes report visions relating to the injury after full recovery of consciousness and these are obviously of very special interest. Thus in paper 4 (Russell 1935):

Another similar case is that of a porter at a picture gallery who had an accident on July 14th, 1934. He was standing on a tramway island when a motor-van passed the island on the wrong side. Though he described himself as the last person to be easily frightened, he evidently threw up his arms when he saw the car, and by so doing was thrown to the ground. He recovered full consciousness in hospital 12 hours later. During the following two weeks he could remember nothing he had done for a period of about ten minutes before the accident occurred. About two weeks after the accident the retrograde amnesia lessened, and he could then remember standing on the tramway island just before the accident. Four months after the accident the period of retrograde amnesia was unaltered, and he had absolutely no recollection of the accident or of the 12 hours which followed. He informed me, however, that for about a week after his admission to hospital he had on many occasions a sudden vision of the huge tyre of a motor lorry bearing down on him while he threw up his arms unable to escape. These visions only occurred during the week following the accident.

Further examples are reported in paper 7 (Russell and Nathan 1946, pp. 287–8).

Driver T's first memory on coming round in hospital was of seeing a horse as in a cloud. He had a very clear idea of the horse; it was a brown cob, and he had a side-view of it. It was galloping with its head up, coming from right to left. There was no cart attached to it; he was unaware of any background of road or surrounding scenery or people or noise. He was unaware of being frightened or of any feeling that an accident was about to occur. This vision at once passed and he was aware of two nurses making his bed. He asked them what had happened, and they told him he had had an accident. He then asked them whether it was anything to do with a horse, and they told him they did not know, but that he had already told them that it occurred through a horse. He himself had no recollection of having told them this. This story of the accident has been confirmed: he did collide with a runaway horse.

Driver L. (*Case* 15207) was involved in a motor car accident in April, 1944. He was sitting next to the driver and has been told that the accident was due to the steering rod breaking. When examined in September, 1944, he had made a good recovery apart from some headache. He had complete R.A. for about twenty minutes, and this amnesia included a special visit by car to a river. The P.T.A. was for three to four days. Under sodium amytal hypnosis five months after the accident he talked freely but no shortening of the R.A. or P.T.A. could be obtained. He did, however, recover an island in the R.A. during which he was sitting in the car reading a letter while they were travelling at about 35 m.p.h. He also thought that he could remember looking up suddenly, but had no recollection of the driver struggling with the steering wheel, nor had he any memory of the visit to the river.

"*Visions*"—About two weeks after the accident he had his first "vision" and he had six of these in all, of which four were during the two months following the injury. The "visions" consisted of the sudden appearance in his right visual field of a man, and especially the man's arms, struggling with the steering wheel of a car. This "vision" lasted for a few seconds. It only occurred while he was completely at rest both mentally and physically, generally while sitting in an easy chair. On the first two occasions of the "vision" he felt frightened, and his "stomach turned over", but in the more recent attacks he recognized the "vision" and there was no associated emotional reaction to it. He is naturally a visualist and has visual dreams during sleep, but has never seen this "vision" during sleep and has no dreams relative to the accident.

Fitter P. (*Case MRC* 232)(Hooper, McGregor and Nathan 1945) "came round" in hospital two and a half days after his accident. He became vaguely aware of the ward surroundings, but at the same time he seemed to hear a confused jumble of voices, shouts and the noise of brakes being applied; he saw two car lights, and had a vivid impression of being dragged along on his back. These sensations lasted for about two minutes and recurred later with a highly unpleasant and terrifying sensation as an aura to an attack which might have been an epileptic equivalent.

In this case, unlike the first three, a part of the hallucination was clearly remembered as occurring before the injury, for he remembered the screech of brakes and his being struck by a car but could never recall being dragged along the road.

These rare cases suggest that during the period of confusion isolated and dramatic events preceding the injury may be registered and retained which cannot be recalled in the normal way, but only in the form of a "vision".

These half-memories are usually visual and may be compared to some observations by research psychologists on the study of showing the patient special material before undergoing electro-shock therapy.

This phenomenon of a half-memory not amenable to the ordinary process of recall might be interpreted as a failure simply of the recalling system, but current physiological studies both in man and animals encourage the idea rather of an incomplete memory trace.

The absence of any emotion in relation to some of these hallucinations of events within the R.A., supports the idea of a lack of completion of the memory trace, for an established memory also establishes a related emotional reaction to it. The quick fading of these visions also favours the conception of an incomplete process that decays for lack of the completing process.

Anomalies of behaviour during traumatic confusion

During the period for which there is subsequently amnesia, that is during the P.T.A. period, certain interesting anomalies of behaviour and conversation were described on p. 19 where it was pointed out that occasionally the patient, while quite confused, may be able to give important information about the accident which is later quite forgotten, but confabulation may confuse the issue.

During the period of confusion following concussion which falls within the P.T.A., speech and behaviour may be so nearly normal that confabulation misleads the unskilled observer. The subject matter for confabulation is usually unconnected with the injury, but in some instances the patient apparently realizes he has had an accident and confabulates with regard to it (see p. 19). This may lead to the patient making false accusations regarding the cause of the injury, as has already been described. A case was reported by C. W. Somerville (1931) in which a doctor motored home a boy who had fallen off his cycle, and the boy subsequently told his parents that the doctor had run him down. Careful questioning in such a case often makes it possible to demonstrate a complete R.A. for the period regarding which the false accusation is being made. In Dr. Somerville's case it subsequently emerged that there was an R.A. for 10 minutes before the accident—the boy had no recollection of leaving home to go on his cycle and his belief therefore was based on confused thoughts and memories of events during the P.T.A. while he was being brought home after the accident.

If, however, after an accident the subject can describe correctly events that immediately preceded the injury, then there is no justification to doubt the reliability of the description given of these happenings provided, of course, that he is not just repeating what he has been told after the injury. This may be of medico-legal importance, as in the Merritt trial (Roughhead 1929) in which an attempt was made with some success to discredit evidence given by Mrs. Merritt of events that occurred just before she was shot in the head. She gave this evidence while conscious some days after the injury.

The amnesic features can only be appreciated in the acute stage of traumatic confusion if the stages of recovering consciousness are appreciated.

Stages in the recovery of consciousness

The stages of recovery of consciousness, and particularly of the mental and speech functions, are of great interest in relation to the subsequent amnesias. The following case record provides a typical illustration of the steps towards recovery in a case of severe head injury (from paper 2, Russell 1932, p. 566).

R.D., a shepherd, aged 27, was admitted to hospital on May 3, 1931, having been thrown off his motor cycle. When examined a few hours later there was no severe shock. He was bleeding from the right ear and was tossing restlessly in bed. He made no attempt to speak and was in a deeply stuporose condition.

May 4—Owing to violent restlessness he was transferred to the ward for incidental delirium, where he had to be strapped in bed. He powerfully resisted any interference and seemed very sensitive when the plantar reflexes were being examined. There was little or no attempt to speak.

May 5—To-day he was fighting hard against the straps which held him down and calling out loudly without using any definite words.

May 9—He greeted me cheerfully with "Good morning, Sir," and shook hands. He talked cheerfully about having to get home to-night. Much of what he said was meaningless, but a few sentences were intelligible. He gave his name correctly, but in reply to a question said, "I've been here two years." Sentences often begun correctly, later became meaningless. "Here, could I go out into the . . ." He almost wept when prevented from getting up, and seemed very annoyed. "Well, I'll come back again," he would say impatiently. "That's no kind of way to . . . now don't you think it." Then, sitting up and waving his arms about, he would argue vehemently but quite meaninglessly with the attendant, and wept when again prevented from getting up. Plantar reflexes were to-day flexor, whereas they had been previously extensor on both sides.

May 19—He was very talkative and emphasized all he said with powerful gestures. His condition was very like that of a talkative and intoxicated person. He argued that he must go home, and boasted freely of his great skill at shearing sheep and catching trout. He promised to give money to the Sister and examiner if they would let him go. He talked incessantly and repeated his arguments over and over again. Most of his sentences were coherent, but a few were meaningless. Like a man who is intoxicated, he paid little or no attention to what was said to him, and would not listen to reason. He had no knowledge of where he was and absolutely no comprehension of his condition. After considerable persuasion he would respond to a simple request, such as "Put out your tongue."

May 25—He was quite changed. He remembered being troublesome in the ward and was now very apologetic. He said he felt very well and strong enough to start work again. He knew where he was and why he was there, and had a normal understanding of his environment. There was no repetition of his former unbalanced talk. He listened to and appreciated all that was said to him. He could now recollect certain events preceding the accident. He remembered driving along the road at a speed of about 35 miles an hour, anxious to get home before dark, and remembered actually colliding with the tar barrel which caused his accident.

Thereafter this patient's recovery was uneventful. When seen seven months later he was physically fit, but his doctor said he was much less reserved than before the accident. He had now no recollection of hitting the tar barrel but remembered events clearly to within a few minutes of the accident. He was unable to remember the number of sheep he counted about six hours before the accident, but otherwise he could find no fault with his memory.

I have made several detailed records of the recovery of speech in cases such as the above and have found that they show remarkable similarity. At first all words are impossible. The first attempt to articulate usually takes the form of a groan or a shout repeated frequently. Then a few words are occasionally uttered. These may be meaningless, but soon a few common phrases are correctly produced. These are often repeated frequently and are usually shouted out loudly. The patient's vocabulary gradually increases. Common phrases are at first all that can be said, but gradually speech becomes more intelligible. There is still, however, a lack of any power of understanding or reason. The patient's incessant talk is mainly repetition. He pays no attention to what is said to him and is quite disorientated. The inhibitions and social training which prompt the average patient to speak with respect to the nurses and doctor are among the last functions to recover, so that he is often impudent to and familiar with his attendants. Subsequent to this stage the recovery of insight, orientation and the usual social habits rapidly follows, and the patient recovers full consciousness and begins to think about events preceding his accident.

Comment

The phenomenon of shrinking retrograde amnesia is often observed during the later stages of recovery from traumatic confusion. The suggestion has been made on p. 63 that this indicates a relative vulnerability of recent memories and points to an automatic strengthening of memories as time passes or to an automatic strengthening of the capacity to recall memories.

Another possibility, however, is simply that during minor states of confusion after trauma (or indeed in old age) the memories that can be recalled depend on features of the memories themselves and that for reasons quite unconnected with their age some old memories are strong and, by being preferentially recalled, upset correct orientation in time (see p. 77).

Another very important aspect of retrograde amnesia is that training experiences during the R.A. period may be preserved as a learned skill although the learning cannot be recalled. Thus case P.A.S. (p. 234) was able to do his work during the transient period of long R.A. although the place of work seemed to be unfamiliar. There seem to be different grades of the learning process. Thus Dr. Honor V. Smith has kindly provided particulars of a soldier who recovered after treatment for tuberculous meningitis. After recovery he had the usual amnesia for most of the illness and a very long R.A. extending for about a year before his illness began. Two years after his illness the R.A. was particularly dense for three months before his illness began. During that period he had been sent on a clerk's training course and he was unable to recall anything about this. However, when shown a photograph of others attending the course, he was able to name many of them correctly. He could also describe some of a typewriting chart from which he was taught during that period.

Various experiments on the recall of material presented before electro-shock treatment have also demonstrated that something is often stored from test material presented during moments that subsequently are found to be in the period of apparently dense R.A.

It seems therefore that the traumatic amnesias we study are concerned with a high-level type of learning that does not correspond with the comparatively simple learning processes concerned with the arrival of relatively simple afferent information. Patients with a permanent severe Korsakoff's syndrome can, it seems, learn by practice some simple tasks.

In 1956 Bender identified the syndrome of isolated episode of confusion with amnesia. These short-lasting 'transient amnesic episodes' are now widely recognized and are thought to be due to ischaemic lesions of the hippocampal region. The amnesic period usually lasts for a few hours, during which the patient may behave normally but is in reality confused and disorientated. Mumenthaler and von Roll (1969), in a remarkable study of fourteen such patients, report that during the amnesic episode the R.A. may be very long—up to several years' duration. After the episode passes there is no obvious R.A. and amnesia only for the episode. This rapid switch from a Korsakoff state to normality puts a different and important emphasis on the connection between a long R.A. and a state of mental confusion. The memory traces seem to be intact but recall is inactivated temporarily, and during this time the patient can recall normally for only a period of a minute after a stimulus is given. Here again we encounter an intimate connection between the ability to hold new information and the whole recalling system, and of course the inevitable state of confusion when these mechanisms are out of action. This further evidence indicates that the shrinking R.A. of the recovering head injury should probably be studied as a corollary of the state of mental confusion. The ability to link one moment of experience with the next seems to be a vital aspect of normality and emphasizes again the physiological significance of the moment at which the period of traumatic amnesia ends. The physiological links between recall, ability to store new information (remember and learn), and the ability to remember events of the moment in their proper order all seem to be fundamental to our study.

5

THE AMNESIAS ASSOCIATED WITH SPECIAL TYPES OF INJURY

Crushing injuries

As has been discussed on p. 6, the study of the mechanisms of concussion has been furthered by the observation that severe crushing injuries of the skull and severe local damage to the brain may occur without any resulting disturbance of consciousness. Such crushing injuries were described in paper 11 (Russell and Schiller 1949, extract from pp. 52–4).

Severe crushing injuries of the head are often fatal, but in those patients who survive this form of injury the absence or slight degree of concussion is usually a striking feature of the clinical picture. Even though the skull may be fractured and the cranial nerves injured, the patient often remains fully conscious. This clinical observation led one of us (W.R.R.) with Denny-Brown (1941) to investigate experimentally the mechanism of cerebral concussion, and we found, as might be expected from clinical experience, that concussion is more readily produced by a blow when the head is free to move and not fixed. In most cases of accidental head injury the head is subjected to a sudden change of momentum which causes the shearing stresses in the brain which have been analysed by Holbourn (1943), and so brilliantly demonstrated experimentally by Pudenz and Sheldon (1946). It seems clear that the common retention of consciousness with crushing injuries of the skull is due to the absence of any sudden change of momentum with an injury of this nature.

Compression of the skull beyond a certain degree will, however, cause loss of consciousness and brain damage by cerebral compression. The term *compression concussion* has been used to denote this form of injury (Denny-Brown and Russell, 1941).

Case Records

Case 1.—J. O'B., a miner, aged 49, was admitted to the Royal Infirmary, Edinburgh, on Jan. 1, 1933, shortly after an accident. He was working in a coal seam 26 inches high when a fall of rock pinned his head to the ground (lateral compression). He remained fully conscious but when released by other workers he was bleeding from the nose and right ear. When examined next day he was fully conscious, and there was little headache. There was a bruise in the left frontal region and extensive subconjunctival haemorrhage in the right eye. He reported having swallowed a lot of blood from his nose: there was blood in the right ear and right facial weakness. Radiographs of the skull failed to show a fracture. By Jan. 29, 1933, there was complete right facial paralysis and complete right sixth-nerve palsy. He was discharged home on Feb. 4, 1933. The cranial nerve palsies recovered slowly, but on Dec. 24, 1933, he fell in an attack of vertigo and fractured the neck of his left femur. In February, 1935, his health was satisfactory, and he was planning to start light work.

Case 2.—T. L., a railway carriage examiner, aged 31, was admitted to the Royal Infirmary, Edinburgh, on July 24, 1933, after an accident in which his head had been crushed between two railway carriages. He remembered all details of the accident and after release was able to walk for five minutes to a house. There was bleeding from the nose and both ears. He was conscious but very shocked on admission to hospital. When examined on July 25, 1933, he was fully conscious, but had severe headache and marked neck rigidity. The left pupil was larger than the right and there was complete left sixth-nerve paralysis. Radiological examination revealed a fissure fracture in the right fronto-temporal region. On Aug. 1, 1933, the cerebrospinal fluid pressure was 100 mm of water and the fluid was deeply blood-stained (33,000 red cells per c.mm) and on standing the supernatant fluid was bright yellow. The white cell count was 314 per c.mm (15 per cent polymorphs). Following lumbar puncture he had a rigor and high fever at night for five days; thereafter he made a gradual recovery and was discharged home on Aug. 17, 1933.

Case 3.—A. C., a labourer, aged 43, had his head and left leg pinned down by heavy oi drums sliding down from a pile. He did not lose consciousness, and he said afterwards that he was most concerned with the immediate pain in his crushed leg, and he shouted for help to be released from the drums as he was unable to extricate himself. He was bleeding from his left ear which, from having a slight previous defect in hearing, became completely deaf. There was a transient left sixth-nerve weakness and an almost complete left facial palsy which was still present one month after the accident. Only special oblique radiograph showed a fracture of the left petrous bone involving the mastoid air cells (Fig. 7). The patient would have been able to resume work within three weeks, but for the fractured leg.

Case 4.—When 22 years of age J. R., a miner, was crushed between two hutches in the mine. He remembers all details of the injury and apparently the crush was bitemporal in direction. There was bleeding from both nostrils and the right ear. When examined seventeen years later (March 11, 1935) he was in fair health but had suffered from headaches at frequent intervals ever since the injury.

Case. 5—J. McN., aged 63, was admitted to the Royal Infirmary, Edinburgh, on Dec. 2, 1936, shortly after an accident. While he was standing between a motor lorry and a wall the lorry moved backwards and pinned his head against the wall. There was no loss of consciousness, and he remembers clearly the acute pain caused by the injury. Blood poured from his right ear, nose, and mouth. On the following day he developed complete left facial paralysis and there was slight deafness of both ears. There was effusion around the right eye with subconjunctival haemorrhage. He had severe headaches for twenty-four hours. X-ray examination demonstrated a fracture in the right temporal bone.

He returned home on Jan. 5, 1937. When seen again on Sept. 6, 1937, he was free from symptoms and the facial paralysis had recovered.

Case 6.—W. G., a pit-boy, aged 15, was caught between two hutches in the mine on Oct. 11, 1937. Consciousness was not disturbed, and he was able to jump aside when the hutches separated. He remembers the severe pain of the crush, and blood poured from both ears and both nostrils. He was admitted to the Royal Infirmary, Edinburgh, the same day. There was pain in the head for a few days only, but radiographs revealed a vertical fracture involving the right parietal, squamous and petrous portions of the temporal bone. There was slight impairment of the sense of smell on the right side, and left facial weakness. He made a quick recovery, and when re-examined on Feb. 7, 1938, he felt quite fit.

Case 7.—J. T., a pit-boy, aged 14½ years, was crushed between hutches on Oct. 11, 1937. He remembers all details of the injury, but was reported to be dazed when admitted to the Royal Infirmary, Edinburgh, a few hours later. There was no x-ray evidence of fracture, but blood escaped from both ears and the nose. Five days later stereoscopic radiographs with the occipito-mental projection failed to show any fracture of the base of the skull. On Oct. 19, 1937, he was feeling fairly well but had diplopia. The left pupil was larger than the right, and reacted normally to light and convergence. The right pupil was inactive to light but contracted slightly on convergence. There was slight limitation of the outward movement of the left eye. On Jan. 5, 1938, the diplopia had recovered and the pupils were normal: he felt quite well and ready to resume work.

Case 8.—E. M., aged 29, while cycling was caught between two motor vehicles and his head was crushed. So horrible did the accident look that he was reported dead in the evening paper of Sept. 29, 1947. But when admitted to the Radcliffe Infirmary, Oxford, he was found to be only moderately concussed, and he regained full consciousness a few hours after the accident.

There was bleeding from the left ear, bilateral deafness of a middle-ear type, bilateral external rectus and bilateral facial palsy, and complete anaesthesia and masticatory paralysis on the right side of the face. There was dysarthria and dysphagia, but no evidence of abnormality of the long cerebrospinal tracts. Radiographs showed a fracture running into the left middle fossa, and an aerocele filling the interpeduncular cisterna.

The hearing in both ears returned (with a scarred drum on the left side). The dysphagia subsided. But he remained somewhat dysarthric and much troubled by the lesions of the right fifth nerve and of both sixth and both seventh nerves.

Case 9.—Rfmn. P., aged 21, was on Dec. 6, 1941, crushed between an army lorry and a girder in a garage. He remembers the impact but nothing more for about twenty minutes, when he remembers being in an ambulance. On recovering consciousness he was found to have extreme dysarthria of a cerebellar type with ataxia of the limbs. The pupils were eccentric, being nearer the nasal edge of the cornea. They were also not quite circular, and there was marked hippus. No other abnormality was noted. X-ray examination revealed an extensive comminuted fracture of the left parietal bone, 10 by 5 cm in size. Eighteen months later his speech was still indistinct. He complained of headaches, irritability, and periods of depression. He had been obliged to give up several jobs.

Case 10.—Gnr. S., aged 29, was on Nov. 10, 1941, examining a gun tyre when the vehicle moved and passed over his head, pinning him to the ground. He remained fully conscious, but was unable to speak, and drummed the ground with his feet to attract attention. There was bleeding from the right nostril for an hour and some headache for twenty-four hours. In hospital he was found to have a complete ophthalmoplegia and blindness of the right eye, with anaesthesia in the distribution of the right supraorbital nerve. He remained fully conscious. The right clavicle was fractured.

X-ray examination revealed fractures of the roof of the right orbit, the right optic foramen, and of the greater wing of the sphenoid.

By April 30, 1942, both the vision in the right eye and the ocular movements had recovered. The right pupil was, however, smaller than the left and inactive to light. As far as the head injury was concerned he had made a good recovery.

Case 11.—Gnr. A. F., aged 24, was on Feb. 11, 1941, travelling in a lorry when it overturned and he was crushed by 100-lb shells it was conveying. Though there was no loss of consciousness and no amnesia, there was bleeding from the nose and weakness of the left sixth and seventh cranial nerves. The left pupil was smaller than the right and there was slight left deafness. He developed pulsating exophthalmos of the left eye, which was cured by ligation of the internal carotid artery first in the neck and later within the skull. Glaucoma of the left eye developed with complete loss of vision. X-ray examination failed to reveal any fracture. A year after the injury he was able to resume light manual work.

Case 12.—2/Lt. S., aged 20, had his head crushed below a Morris 8-h.p. motor car when the jack slipped. The rear axle pinned his head to the ground. He remained fully conscious while a friend lifted the car, and he was then able to get out and to stand up with blood pouring from his nose and right ear and from a cut on the left forehead. He noticed double vision while being taken to hospital. There was slight weakness of the right lateral rectus muscle, depression of the right corneal reflex, right facial paresis, and slight right deafness. Radiographs revealed a fissure fracture of the anterior part of the left squamous temporal bone which ran vertically upwards to the squamo-parietal junction, and downward into the base of the skull.

He made a good recovery and returned to duty two months after the injury.

Case 13.—Spr. S., aged 28, was on July 1, 1941, working under a truck when the jack slipped, and his head was pinned between the front axle and the ground. He was rendered deeply unconscious and had amnesia for fifteen days. There was bleeding from left parietal and right occipital wounds, but none from the nose or ears. The cerebrospinal fluid fourteen hours after the injury contained blood; the pressure was 180 mm of water. The right pupil was larger than the left, and the left arm and leg were slightly spastic with a left extensor plantar response.

X-ray examination revealed no fracture of the skull. Some weakness of the left side persisted, but he made a fair recovery and resumed light work nine months later.

Case 14.—Gnr. M., aged 30, was on May 6, 1942, caught between two heavy motor vehicles moving very slowly. He did not lose consciousness at any time, but a bolt on one of the vehicles caused a depressed fracture of the right temporal bone. This was operated on the same day: the dura was intact. There was also a cut in the left occipital region. The only abnormal physical signs were nystagmus and the right pupil was larger than the left. He made a good recovery apart from some headaches reported on a follow-up report dated Oct. 13, 1943.

Case 15.—Pte. O. M., aged 20, overturned a truck he was driving on Feb. 26, 1942. While crawling out the truck settled on his head. There was no loss of consciousness or amnesia. Radiographs revealed a depressed fracture in the left parieto-temporal region.

He made a good recovery, and a year later was reported free from symptoms but serving a sentence in prison.

Discussion of Clinical Cases

The cause of the crushing injury in these fifteen cases was as follows:

	Cases
Head caught between hutches	3
Head crushed by fall of rock in mine	1
Crush between railway carriages	1
Crush between backing lorry and wall	2
Crush between 2 motor vehicles	2
Crush under axle of motor vehicle	2
Crush under overturned lorry	1
Crush under oil drums	1
Crush under several 100-lb shells	1
Crush under gun-wheel	1

The signs of skull injury were:

X-ray evidence of fracture	10
Bleeding from the ears	9
bilateral	3
Bleeding from the nose	9

Fourteen of the fifteen cases showed clinical or x-ray evidence of skull fracture. Nevertheless the absence of concussion was a marked feature of most cases. Indeed all remained fully conscious without amnesia except three of the fifteen in which there was amnesia for twenty minutes, a few hours, and fifteen days respectively.

All except three cases showed cranial nerve involvement as follows:

			Cases
Second cranial nerve	.	.	2(one optic chiasm)
Fifth cranial nerve	.	.	3(upper division)
Sixth cranial nerve	.	.	8(bilateral in one)
Pupillary changes .	.	.	6
Ophthalmoplegia	.	.	1
Deafness	.	.	5(bilateral in two)
Dysarthria	.	.	2

One patient developed a carotico-cavernous aneurysm, one a severe mid-brain syndrome, and one an aerocele. In two cases sub-arachnoid haemorrhage was demonstrated.

The clinical features are therefore quite striking, for there is commonly clear evidence of fracture of the base of the skull and injury to cranial nerves without any of the loss of consciousness or concussion which so constantly accompanies the common forms of accidental head injury.

Focal lesions

These are described in paper 14 (Russell 1959, pp. 75–6).

The wounds of modern warfare are often caused by small metal fragments travelling at high velocity. When these strike the skull they may cut into the brain, or, if tangential, may glance away from the skull. In either event contact with the skull often has a locally explosive effect so that a shower of bone fragments is forced into the brain below the site of injury for a distance of a few centimetres.

These wounds may, of course, be grossly destructive, but among those patients who survive are many with small wounds confined to one area of brain. These patients provide a unique opportunity for the study of focal brain lesions (Russell, 1951). Thus 75 per cent. of 700 cases of brain wound had focal signs of brain damage after wounding, which included disorders such as paralysis of one or more limbs, hemianopia, and aphasia.

Of special interest, however, is the large number of such cases in which the penetrating wound of the brain causes no disturbance of consciousness, and the patient can describe in detail the moment of wounding and the sudden development of, say, paralysis or aphasia. This is in striking contrast to the loss of consciousness which occurs in acceleration concussion, the difference being that in penetrating wounds the brain is not subjected to the general neuronal commotion of acceleration concussion. Thus in over 25 per cent. of penetrating war wounds of the brain in patients who survived, there was no amnesia for the injury, and in a further 20 per cent. there was amnesia (P.T.A.) for less than one hour.

These are mostly wounds of the cerebral hemispheres, and it is of some interest to look for any area of the cortex which has a greater influence on causing amnesia for the wound than other areas. Russell (1948a) found such an area in the left temporal lobe, but this may be connected in some way with the aphasic phenomena which accompany such a wound.

Aphasia disorganizes many so-called mental processes, as indeed is to be expected if we accept the evidence that man's power of thought cannot develop without training also his speech faculties in both sensory and motor aspects.

Comment

These figures emphasize the fact that sudden destruction of small cortical areas of the cerebral hemispheres often results in no disturbance of consciousness. Thus the soldier with a brain wound may remember quite clearly going blind, paralysed, or aphasic according to the part of the brain injured.

On p. 58 the effects of certain deep wounds of the brain are considered, but as regards the usual localized type of cortical and subcortical missile wound, there is some evidence that certain wounds of the left hemisphere tend to cause a longer P.T.A. than do wounds of the right hemisphere.

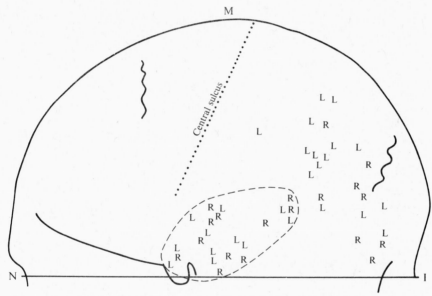

FIG. 1. The site of the brain wounds studied of the right (R) and left (L) cerebral hemispheres, which all led to permanent damage to one optic radiation without injury to the sensori-motor system.

The following extract is from paper 10 (Russell 1948*b*, pp. 97–99).

The study of the duration of amnesia in focal brain wounds throws further light on this matter. In a group of 250 cases of gun-shot wounds of the brain which penetrated the cerebrum for a distance of over 3 cms. there were 56 in which there was no amnesia relative to the incident. There were a number of frontal, Rolandic, anterior temporal and posterior occipital wounds in this group, and some of the right parieto-temporal region, but there seemed to be a lack of wounds of the left posterior parieto-temporal region in which there was no amnesia.

More detailed evidence regarding this is provided by comparing wounds which injured the optic radiations on the right and left sides of the brain. Fig. 1 gives the site of wounds of this type. The criteria used for inclusion in this group are that the wound damaged the optic radiation but caused no pronounced permanent loss of sensation or weakness of the limbs of the contralateral side.

Wounds penetrating the skull within 5 cms. of the midline are excluded in order to avoid most of the calcarine wounds. In all other respects the cases are unselected. This figure charts the site of wounding in 45 cases, 19 to the right side and 26 to the left side of the brain. The method of charting is by measurement of the site of the wound from skull X-rays according to a method described elsewhere (Russell, 1947). In Table II the prolonged amnesia commonly observed in wounds of this part of the left cerebral hemisphere is clearly shown. This contrast between the two hemispheres is even more striking in Table III which charts the wounds which penetrated straight into the brain over the anterior part of the optic radiation. Though the number of cases in this group is small I am told that the difference between right and left is highly significant from the statisticians' calculations.

TABLE II.—*Duration of Amnesia in Cases Charted on Fig.* 1. *Comparison Between Wounds of the Left and Right Side of the Brain*

Duration of Post-traumatic Amnesia (45 *Cases*)

Side of Wound	Nil	<1 hour	<24 hours	>24 hours	Total Cases
Right . . .	7	5	1	6	19
Left . . .	2	2	3	19	26

An interesting point emerges from these tables for if the cases in Table III are subtracted from those in Table II the resulting table shows no significant difference between right and left. The statistical significance therefore of Table II depends on it containing the cases charted in Table III. Further we have failed to find evidence of any difference as regards amnesia between right and left sided wounds in other parts of the brain, but this matter will be analysed more accurately at a later date.

TABLE III.—*Duration of Amnesia in Cases Charted Within the Dotted Line on Fig.* 1. *Comparison Between Wounds of the Right and Left Side of the Brain*

Duration of Post-traumatic Amnesia (22 *Cases*)

Side of Wound	Nil	<1 hour	<24 hours	>24 hours	Total Cases
Right . . .	6	2	1	2	11
Left . . .	1	—	1	9	11

These observations do not of course mean that the cortex overlying the anterior part of the optic radiation is a memory centre and indeed there are cases of cortical injury here without amnesia. All these wounds penetrated the white matter far enough to damage the optic radiation and presumably injured association paths between parietal, temporal and occipital lobes.

They do, however, strongly suggest that the white matter in this situation normally plays an essential part in the establishment of those neuronal circuits which are established by current events in such a way that they can be subsequently recalled to memory.

One must of course distinguish between this disturbance of current recording and any permanent loss of remote or recent memory, and I am not yet able to give you information regarding the permanent effect on memory of wounds in this situation. There was, however, in most of these left temporal wounds some persistent aphasia in which difficulty in finding the right word was usually a feature, and it should be noted that difficulty in finding words is a form of remote memory loss. All these patients were of course severely aphasic immediately after wounding, and were often reported to be conscious, but there is no association of early aphasia and long amnesia in wounds elsewhere in the dominant hemisphere. It is only the dysphasic cases who have wounds in this situation which show almost always this long amnesia after injury.

These observations indicate the need to study disease of the dominant hemisphere in a fuller manner than is provided simply by observing the effects on the speech mechanism. The pattern of human behaviour, memory and speech are all so closely linked that the study of aphasia alone is apt to be misleading.

I am particularly indebted to Dr R. B. Fisher for his statistical analysis of the tables.

Comment

These wounds of the temporal lobe may inactivate the underlying hippo-campal area and these observations suggest a leading role for the left side of the brain unless, of course, the consequences of the associated aphasia have an overwhelming effect on the limbic system for reasons that are unknown.

Of special interest are a group of cases in which a small metal missile fragment reaches or crosses the mid-line in the region of the third ventricle, for these have a special tendency to cause a severe temporary or permanent amnesic disorder. These are described in paper 17 (Russell 1963, p. 43) which also summarizes existing knowledge on the question.

I think it is important to keep in mind that the clinical neurologist must always have an important contribution to make in the study of brain mechanisms. Thus we are very familiar with the various varieties of amnesia which appear in the clinic, and they are of great scientific interest. The capacity to memorize something of *current* events is essential for orientation and sanity, and when this capacity is impaired by illness or disease for which Delay (1949) used the term *amnésie de mémoration*, many striking psychological consequences result. In some instances of this "fixation amnesia" there is a striking preservation of remote memories, and yet it should be noted that these preserved and accessible remote memories were originally laid down with the aid of a neuronal system which is out of action when there is *amnésie de mémoration*, as in Korsakoff's syndrome.

The process of holding new material is very dynamic in that it requires time for its operation to continue long after the event occurred which is to be recorded. This is evident from the study of retrograde amnesia after head injury or electric convulsion therapy (E.C.T.), and also from a study of the interference with learning in rats by E.C.T. given after their training runs (Gerard, 1961).

It has become very apparent in recent years that the limbic system is closely concerned with memorizing. Destruction of the corpora mammillaria as in Wernicke's encephalopathy or of the hippocampus on both sides as in some forms of encephalitis or after surgical removal, leads to *amnésie de mémoration* with retention of old memories. It is also of great interest that Green and Petsche (1961) have demonstrated that the hippocampal activity amounts to a "virtual generating" station for neuronal activity.

The limbic system is closely connected with mid-brain activating mechanisms concerned with survival and other basic necessities. Here there seems to be a driving force which encourages the retention elsewhere in the brain of some few of the vast mass of items which bombard the nervous system from the special senses.

Thus both the clinical and physiological studies demonstrate a highly dynamic mechanism in relation to the hippocampus—a structure which is very much concerned with establishing memories throughout the brain.

There is much that is unknown about the limbic structures concerned with these generating and dynamic processes, but it seems highly probable that damage to limbic mechanisms on one side only will not cause this memorizing defect and that the lesion must be bilateral. The part played by the thalamic nuclei, the hypothalamus, the fornix, the septal nuclei, or the hippocampal commissure is not known, so that there is still much interest in the anatomical aspects. What is more, I understand that the anatomical pathways by which the limbic system could drive the brain are not really well-known.

Korsakoff's syndrome occurs in tuberculous meningitis, 3rd ventricle tumors and perhaps in lesions of the fornix. It has also been described in cases of war wounds in which metal fragments of shell or mortar have penetrated to the region of the 3rd ventricle, and from our Oxford collection of 1,000 cases of brain wounds I have found eight such cases in which *amnésie de mémoration* was a marked and persistent clinical feature. The most striking cases were those in which a small metal fragment entered the skull and brain near the sagittal line in the occipital or frontal region and passed respectively forwards or backwards near the sagittal plane but usually crossing it and apparently traversing the position of the fornix and septum lucidum. These wounds often caused neither hemiplegia, hemianopia nor aphasia, but sneaked in (as it were) to damage centrally placed structures without any involvement of the major tracts which we as neurologists are constantly testing in patients with brain disease. In some instances the confusion caused by *amnésie de mémoration* seemed to lead to psychotic behavior requiring admission to psychiatric units. Tracings of the radiographs of the skulls of these patients present many interesting anatomical problems for the skull radiographs in each case show the small point of entry and the position of the metal fragment.

6

PHYSIOLOGY OF MEMORY

PAPER 13 (Russell 1958) was the Address as President of the Neurological Section of the Royal Society of Medicine, and is here reported in full.

It is hard to realize that only 200 years ago the brain was still thought by our forefathers to consist of a concoction of spirits which might be pure and tranquil, or riotous and evil. It was no wonder that the highly complex human mind was considered to be a thing apart from this squashy organ. During the past 100 years, however, the astonishing complexity of the central nervous system (C.N.S.) has been slowly unfolded until its structural mysteries have become even harder to understand than say the so-called mental processes of our friends! This state of affairs has inevitably caused a revolution in man's attitude to his C.N.S., and indeed there seems to be little limit to what this structure might be capable of.

As examples of the changing concepts regarding the C.N.S., I propose to discuss briefly a few of the physiological processes which seem to be concerned with memory, but I should first point out that a certain amount of speculation is unavoidable in discussing a subject about which we know so little.

There seem to be two particularly important aspects of the development of C.N.S. patterns, to which I should like to refer. There is first the apparently fundamental tendency for nerve cells to repeat patterns of activity, so that all reactions have a strong tendency to form arrangements which are repeated whenever possible, and around which more elaborate responses are built. The tendency to repeat seems to be one of the most powerful features of all nervous system activity. The physiological basis for this is of great interest and will be considered later.

The activity of the mature C.N.S. usually falls into well-worn patterns which have formed during the years of development. These furrows of habit become first ruts to guide and then, chains which control our responses to a greater or lesser degree. These bonds of habit affect simple motor performances very strongly so that our very movements assume a unique character: thus the constancy of our handwriting must be a source of wonder and thankfulness to every banker. This capacity to repeat a previous response is clearly an essential part of the physiology of memory.

The second of these particularly important aspects is the capacity of all forms of animal life to encourage or discourage a response according to whether it appears to be advantageous or disadvantageous to the organism.

In the highly developed C.N.S. of man and mammals this system is probably thrown into action at birth by powerful afferents from the infant's viscera and orifices, especially the mouth, but this is soon elaborated into an ever more complex system in which frontohypothalamic mechanisms play an important part. This might be referred to as a *personal reaction* in which what we call *feeling* becomes a prominent feature. This reaction also shows a strong tendency to repetition, and is clearly concerned with the development of the individual feeling response to circumstances.

Although the studies of Freud and his followers have sometimes strayed from the path of reality, yet their insistence on the importance of the earliest infantile responses in relation to the development of future characteristics of the individual is in accord with the background on which what I have called the personal response seems to develop. This appears to me to provide a powerful link between psychology and physiology, which are still somewhat artificially separated from each other. Certainly this personal reaction to events itself forms patterns of response, or habits which seem to lay the foundations on which the individual's characteristics are formed.

From the point of view of memory itself, this personal response is of special importance as it helps to ensure that items which it considers to be advantageous are remembered, and of course, from the point of view of learning, the wish to learn is vital, and presumably represents the personal reaction to what is unknown.

Here then are two striking features of C.N.S. activity—the urge to repeat and the capacity to facilitate what is advantageous—and it is especially with the first of these that we are concerned in studying memory.

Ever since anatomists (including Ramon y Cajal) discovered that the C.N.S. is built up of neurones, it has been realized that much must depend on the properties of these units, and the manner by which they form synaptic connexions with each other.

It is therefore of great importance from the point of view of our subject that neurophysiologists have, in recent years, demonstrated that transmission from one cell to another is greatly augmented if there has been preceding activity across this connexion. This effect has been shown by experiment to operate exclusively in the presynaptic apparatus (Eccles, 1953; Granit, 1955). This is evidence regarding a neuronal mechanism which can be correlated with the tendency to repeat which permeates all levels of C.N.S. activity.

Physiological Mechanism of the Ability to Repeat

In attempting to provide a working hypothesis for the most primitive type of memory—the simple repetition of a reaction—we must appreciate that most cells of the C.N.S. are in a state of constant, if somewhat random, activity in which they discharge spontaneously day and night, often at a high rate along the processes which communicate with other nerve cells (Young, 1946). The afferent stimuli which lead to reaction or action, are not therefore thrown into a mechanism which is idly waiting for something to do, but into one which is already busily occupied. It is equally evident, however, that this complicated neuronal activity is extremely sensitive to outside (afferent) influences. Apparently the neuronal pool can be alerted to make responses which take priority over spontaneous activity, but a trained and attentive C.N.S. will direct new arrivals into well-established channels, so that if a certain response has in the past followed a given experience, there is every likelihood that this response will be repeated in the future to the same stimulus, until it acquires a remarkable degree of constancy and automaticity.

Even the simplest C.N.S. response involves a vast number of repetitions in the physiological sense; thus the cells involved may perhaps discharge at the rate of

500 per second for several seconds during the height of the response, and may then settle down to relatively slow spontaneous 40–50 per second which causes no overt effect and yet may play a part in preserving the pattern of response.

Simple Learning Processes

The development of constancy in this response constitutes a learning process and in many instances a response seems to be learned quite quickly. Apart from brief interruptions, the neurones concerned continue their spontaneous discharges, and it seems natural to consider that *these spontaneous discharges tend to be directed into the paths opened up by the learned response.* Having learned to walk or cycle one never forgets, not because some pattern is hidden away in a mysterious memory centre, but because the spontaneous activity of the neurones concerned maintains and indeed strengthens the once-established pattern of the response. This mechanism is so remarkably effective that the task once learned may be executed better after an interval of apparent neglect, and the suggestion made is that the C.N.S. maintains what is learned by spontaneous discharges of the cells which are "exercising" as it were, through the neuronal pattern established when the skill was first acquired (Russell, 1948a).

In other words the establishment of the original pattern for the response also established the direction in which the spontaneously occurring activity would tend to flow, and this in its turn would strengthen itself and thus maintain and consolidate the capacity of the organism to repeat, retain and strengthen the skill.

In this sense therefore and unbeknown to the individual, the C.N.S. practises its learned skills and other memories throughout life.

This raises interesting possibilities for there may well be circumstances in which the unconscious activity of the C.N.S. provides a more effective form of training than does actual practice; and, of course, it is intriguing to speculate on the part which this mechanism may play in assisting the mental clarification which often results from putting aside a complicated problem from one's conscious thought for a few days or hours.

Here, however, I am jumping to the conclusion that the memory of a physical task and of a so-called mental problem are basically dependent on the same physiological mechanisms.

Structural Changes at Synapses

The physiological mechanism whereby an active synapse becomes facilitated for future use is not fully understood, but there is some evidence to suggest that physical changes may play a part. Thus the synaptic knobs on the surface of anterior horn cells may, in response to great activity, get larger (Eccles, 1953), and recent work raises some interesting possibilities about a somewhat similar process in the inter-fibre synapses of the cortex. For long there has been something of a mystery about inter-fibre transmission in the cortex but studies described by Bok (1956) suggest a plausible explanation. He has found that 90% of the cerebral cortex consists of spaces which separate nerve cells, glial cells and blood vessels. In this space an immense number of nerve fibres cross each other in various directions, and this fibre density remains much the same in different layers of the cortex, and indeed as between man and animals. The distance which separates crossing nerve fibres is also remarkably constant, and this separation of one fibre from another is apparently maintained by a foam-like structure of spheres whose diameter is about 5μ. It is suggested therefore that fibre synapses depend partly just on the distance which separates fibres from each other. In other words close crossings are facilitated synapses.

A further clue to this is probably provided by a study of the spikes (gemmuli) which appear on the dendrites of cortical pyramidal-type cells. Bok has demonstrated that the gemmuli on a dendrite are, on the whole, separated from each other by a regular distance (2.5μ). This corresponds to the distance apart of the points where crossing fibres would come in close contact with the dendrites on the above arrangement of foam particles. It seems therefore that every spike on the dendrites may become a close-crossing synapse. Further, the development of the gemmuli greatly enhances the effectiveness of the close-crossing synapse by further approximating the crossing fibres. Indeed this increase in size of the fibre at the point of crossing almost (and perhaps entirely) eliminates the space between the crossing fibres. In this simple way the effectiveness of the synapse receives the maximum enhancement.

The development of these gemmuli is presumably a physical change which results from the activity of the synapses concerned, and plays an important part in enhancing their activity. Tremendous multiplication of these occurs during the first two years of life. The crossing at the gemmuli suggests a very firmly-established type of close-crossing synapse, but it may be assumed that simpler mechanisms of enhancement occur without the formation of so much physical change.

In any case the available physiological knowledge suggests that patterns of behaviour depend on the establishment of functional changes at the synapses and not in the cell body. When we laboriously learn to walk we establish a pattern of reaction which probably differs only in the degree of complexity from the higher forms of memory. This conception is important for it suggests that memory, far from depending on passive changes in nerve cells, is a very active process, and becomes lost only when the neurones concerned cease to discharge along the pathways once facilitated. The student of the brain must often be astounded by the complexity of function involved in the simplest mental process, and yet the complexity of the mechanisms involved in voluntary movement is equally astonishing. It is safe to say that if we could understand fully the mechanisms involved in learning the patterns of voluntary motor activity we would be more than half-way towards understanding the physiology of thought processes.

There has sometimes been a tendency to look for some special area of the brain into which all memories could be filed, but this has always seemed to me to be a highly improbable conception. Thus the memory of a physical skill must surely be contained in all parts and levels of the C.N.S. which influence the performance of the skill. Memory of a skill and capacity to repeat it are to some extent one and the same, and the same principle should apply to the higher forms of memory.

Another quality of C.N.S. activity is its capacity to effect a series of responses in a certain order and sequence, and this is a very constant feature of learned responses. From the physiological point of view various phenomena have been demonstrated which introduce delays from one cell to another, but apart from this, the time and sequence patterns of these reactions are little understood. In general, however, there is a striking tendency in all C.N.S. activity for one response to be followed by another, and indeed many motor performances of skill depend almost entirely on reactions which can only occur as a sequence to the first action.

There is also the capacity to co-ordinate one motor memory with another: thus a bandsman remembers both how to walk and how at the same time to play the drum. Presumably our capacity to associate one memory with another at a high level differs again only in complexity with such sensorimotor reactions.

A poem or a piece of music is most easily remembered as a sequence which follows the beginning, and in the highest forms of memory, those with exceptional power in this direction depend largely on a vast capacity of associating memories with each other, this seems to represent a vastly complex type of the simpler ability for one motor reaction to be followed by another.

The recognition of the familiar is an important aspect of memory. A familiar or unfamiliar sight must project in the same pattern on the visual cortex. Most of those patterns are promptly extinguished, but if some attention is aroused, then the familiar is quickly recognized, presumably because the pattern is entering facilitated circuits. Familiar patterns often stimulate a personal feeling of contentment. On the other hand a highly unfamiliar pattern of sound or sight often acts as a strongly alerting reaction with the personal response of fear. These interesting facets of memory are of special interest, as feeling responses to the familiar and unfamiliar may be abolished in animals by certain temporal lobe excisions.

Phantom Limbs

The study of phantom limbs in amputees provides some interesting examples of sensorimotor memory. It is natural that the brain should interpret sensations from the cut nerves as originating in the missing limb. The brain has been trained for many years to interpret these sensations in this way. But if a child should lose a limb in the early months of life, no phantom will develop as the opposite parietal lobe has not yet developed a strong association with the limb.

In many amputees the phantom sensations disappear after a few months. In some, however, after an interval of perhaps twenty years, a painful condition develops in the stump, and once again severe pains are experienced in the phantom. This is a remarkable example of the preservation of an entirely neglected sensorimotor memory. Even more remarkable is that the phantom pain may revive memory of a pain which was felt severely before the limb was amputated (Russell and Spalding, 1950).

In this connexion it is of interest to note that wounds of the parietal lobe of the brain may abolish appreciation of the position of contralateral limbs in relation to the rest of the body (Brain, 1950)—the so-called loss of body image; and in contrast an epileptic aura originating in the parietal lobe may occasionally be a strong phantom sensation in an opposite limb—a forceful distortion of the body image mechanism (Russell, 1951).

The Hippocampal System

There is plenty of evidence to indicate that the hippocampal system is very much involved in this mechanism of memory and recognition of the familiar. Removal of the hippocampus and anterior temporal lobes on both sides causes a remarkable state as Scoville and Milner report (1957). They found that in patients so treated the incidents of daily life were forgotten as quickly as they occurred. Yet details of childhood were well remembered. A somewhat similar result follows disease of the region of the mammillary bodies as in Korsakoff's psychosis, and these bodies form an essential link in the hippocampal system.

Of special interest in this connexion are the temporal-lobe fits which cause an intense sense of familiarity for in this type of focal fit all that is happening seems as if it had happened in the same way before. No other part of the brain stimulates a sense of intense familiarity or *déjà vu* sensation and it seems likely that the hippo-campus is concerned. The focal epileptic fit often caricatures the function of the part of the brain affected so that the occurrence of such fits from the temporal lobe confirms the importance of this region for the physiological reaction which is needed to facilitate neuronal patterns in such a way as to enable an event to be remembered, and to become familiar.

In Korsakoff's syndrome also there is a remarkable dissociation between remote memory and remembering of current events. For it seems as though these remote memories were learned originally with the assistance of a mechanism now out of order, and new learning becomes impossible, though the earlier results are still available. The mechanism that is now out of order was probably the one used to establish originally what is preserved.

This separation of function is also seen in many other states of disordered brain function such, for example, as occur during recovery from concussion. It seems that the mechanism of adding to memories—the recording of events—is more complex and relatively vulnerable, while what was added to memory before the disorder of the mechanism remains relatively secure.

In Korsakoff's syndrome there is plenty of evidence to indicate that an important link in the hippocampal system is broken, for the corpora mammillaria show gross changes and their relations with the hippocampus are so close that their inactivation might be expected to put the system out of action.

It is not unduly fanciful, therefore, to consider that the hippocampus plays an important part in both memory and learning processes. It certainly has free con-nexions with all parts of the cortex, and such a major contribution to thought and behaviour would give it a role well worthy of its great development in man and animals. Yet, although concerned with learning, it probably plays little part in actually storing what has been learned. Its action on the cortical mechanism concerned with visual memory, for example, must be a boosting, feed-back or re-playing mechanism. And, in addition, it might contribute to the essential stimulation of associated ideas and feelings which are so important in consolidating memories.

It is of great interest to study those parts of the brain from which formed visual hallucinations may occur as part of an epileptic process. Dr. Whitty and I (Russell and Whitty, 1955) found that these might occur not only in temporal lobe injuries but also in parieto-occipital lesions. This suggests that both sites are intimately concerned with visual memory; the parieto-occipital region being the region where the main pattern of facilitated circuits lies, and the temporal lobe being concerned perhaps through the hippocampal system in boosting these mechanisms.

These posterior lesions may cause hallucinations of remembered scenes as described by Robinson and Watt (1947), and from wounds further forward in the parietal lobe there may be, as already mentioned, phantom sensations (Russell, 1951) which represent a distortion of the memory of the position of the contralateral limbs in relation to the body image. The disappearance of visual memory and of dreaming (Humphrey and Zangwill, 1951) have been reported in destructive lesions of this part of the brain.

Study of the effects of head injury or senile changes on memory also demonstrate the special vulnerability of recent memories, and indeed it seems that many memories are strengthened with the passage of time regardless of their importance to the individual. This is what one would expect if memory depends on synaptic facilitation of neuronal circuits, which continue to strengthen themselves whether we are interested in them or not.

Hallucinations

Hallucinations provide an interesting study of a disordered memory mechanism. Visual hallucinations are generally of objects which are recognized by virtue of previously acquired knowledge. Thus in delirium tremens the victim is in no doubt as to the type of animals he sees for their appearances are quite familiar to him.

Many individuals with a strong visual sense can develop a special capacity to see things in their mind's eye. This is a simple physiological phenomenon, which may result in artistic productions. Some forms of modern art seem to depend on a cultivated capacity for hallucinatory phenomena to occur in relation to certain feelings. The idea, however, that these haphazard visual images are worth reproducing as works of art seems to me to be based on a misconception of their physiological significance. The artist seems to think that these phenomena are emerging from some unique storehouse of his personal genius, but, on the contrary, the available evidence suggests more that they represent a confused glimpse of fragmentary repetitions of previous thought or reactions.

Hallucinations during illness are likely to be based on remote memories around which there were at one time strong emotional feelings. Thus a woman with delirium tremens may scream with terror at pink mice on the walls, and yet it may have been many years previously that she last experienced an emotional reaction of fear in relation to mice.

A middle-aged doctor while experiencing an infective disease causing an encephalopathy developed some hallucinations which were, in general, of featureless buildings, but somewhat to his surprise, these hallucinations included an illustration from an anatomy textbook which had interested him greatly when he was a young medical student many years previously.

Of special interest are hallucinations of self (Dewhurst and Pearson, 1955), as they tend to be of head and shoulders as would often have been seen in a mirror, and no doubt this appearance has also at one time, perhaps many years previously, aroused an undue amount of interest in the person concerned.

The various visual and auditory memories with their associated emotional responses are contained chiefly in different areas of the cerebral hemispheres, but during hallucinosis the stimulus to uncontrolled activity seems to come from some central system which plays back excessively to the regions such as the parieto-occipital region which is so much concerned with visual memory. The actual hallucinations which appear must depend on many chance factors just as occurs in dreams which, no doubt, make use of a similar mechanism. Indeed hallucinations and dreams are similar in many respects.

The traumatic amnesias are of great interest in relation to our subject (Russell and Nathan, 1946). It is now generally agreed that the concussive effect of a closed head injury is a direct physical disturbance of neuronal function, which leads to a paralysis of brain function.

The gradual recovery of mental processes after head injury provides a vivid picture of the return of first, the less complex, and last, the more complex mechanisms. In this connexion it is informative to realize that current events are not remembered until the recovery of brain function is more or less complete.

During recovery of consciousness it is of special interest to study the commonly occurring phenomenon of shrinkage in the retrograde amnesia. This is best observed in severe cases with slow recovery over a period of several days or weeks. During such recovery recent memories may be so severely lost that the patient thinks himself to be some years younger, and expects the environment and date to be appropriate for that age. Further, if the injury is of such severity as to cause some permanent loss of things previously learned, then this loss is most likely to affect recently acquired knowledge or skills.

Thus in all traumatic or disease processes of the brain there is evidence that recently acquired memories are most vulnerable, while remote memories are often remarkably resistant to disease or trauma. This is therefore a fundamental feature of cerebral dissolution, and can, I think, be explained on the basis put forward that memories depend on synaptic facilitations which strengthen automatically as time passes. Early childhood memories may be relatively indelible for the further reason that the physical changes consequent on prolonged facilitation at a synapse no doubt develop most readily in the child's brain.

The occurrence almost invariably of a short period of retrograde amnesia after recovering from concussion is of course of very special importance, for it clearly indicates that the establishment of a memory, even of the most vivid and emotionally tinged type, requires a period of one or two seconds of normal brain activity, if it is to survive the paralysing effect of concussion. This seems to be a very short time but one second is quite a long time from the neurophysiological point of view.

Of special interest are the occasional visual hallucinations soon after recovering consciousness after head injury. These may be concerned with dramatic events which fall within the period of retrograde amnesia (Russell, 1935; Russell and Nathan, 1946). These visions are only half memories and are soon lost. There is no associated feeling in regard to them, and this can presumably be correlated with their not having been played on by hippocampal and emotional mechanisms.

We might here almost guess that the hippocampal system has to play back to the parieto-occipital region for a period of seconds before even a vivid visual experience can be established as a faint memory. If the cells concerned discharge at the rate of up to 500 per second one gets a rough estimate of how long this effect requires to come through.

It is, of course, even more remarkable that this mechanism of remembering is so efficient that many victims of moderately severe head injuries remember clearly the events which occurred say 10 seconds before the injury. This suggests that the neuronal activity even during the period of traumatic confusion continues to strengthen its memories through its spontaneous activity.

The time factor is only one of many which are concerned with memory. For example, the factor of attention seems to be perhaps the most important of all, for afferents pouring in from the special sense seem to be extinguished automatically, unless they arouse what Pavlov called the "What is it?" reaction.

Further the gradual strengthening of a memory with the passage of time depends on its remaining relatively isolated, and not becoming confused by a large number of closely similar memories, as I have previously pointed out (Russell, 1948a). An experience is not so easily recalled when it ceases to be unique, but becomes confused by scores of very similar memories.

In conclusion, I can only draw a somewhat terrifying picture of thousands of millions of nerve cells all discharging throughout life at high speed, by day and by night to maintain the synaptic patterns on which our memories depend. The very thought of such a mechanism must fill us with a feeling of incredulity. Certainly it makes one tired to think of, but then mental tiredness is itself a remarkable phenomenon.

If our memories are, in fact, facilitated neuronal circuits which never rest, how can we prevent them from constantly disturbing our lives? Thus if the memory of how to swim involves circuits which never rest, why are we not constantly waving our arms and legs around in response to this constant activity?

The answer may lie in a study of what happens to nearly all impulses reaching the nervous system, for it has become quite evident that only a minute fraction of say visual afferents from the retina are "seen" at all. It seems that nearly all afferents to the C.N.S. are immediately extinguished by a process of inhibition. How can this come about? The neurophysiologist will naturally think of the recently described recurrent twigs from the axons of pyramidal cells which have a powerful influence on an inhibitory system connected with the cells described by Renshaw (1946). It is thus quite possible that every pyramidal type of cell has its own cut-out system. In this way it becomes conceivable that our memory neuronal patterns can remain constantly active without reaching what we call consciousness.

What enables us to think of one of our memories or to remember something we see or hear, seems to depend on some general alerting process, and we might here even use the term centrencephalic system as visualized by Penfield.

A friend of mine, a research worker of exceptional originality, told me that if a ticking clock stopped while he was engaged in some mental activity unrelated to the clock, he realized that something had happened and his first memory was of the clock ticking before it had stopped, and he estimated that he would remember about 5 seconds of ticking before it ceased.

Thus it seems that the change from ticking to non-ticking alerted the hearing side of the brain, and that this enabled the memory of recent ticks to be recaptured before they were extinguished like the memory of all other ticks. It is well known that those in charge of running machinery of any kind are alerted by any change in the running sounds.

Also if one suddenly starts listening to what someone is saying, it may be possible to recapture the word or two before alerting began, usually not enough to avoid getting into trouble for not listening to what is being said.

In any case it seems evident that we rely on nearly all the afferents arriving at the C.N.S. being promptly extinguished, and one might even guess that a disturbance of this balance might play a part in the aetiology of traumatic epilepsy.

It must be obvious from this brief address that there are more unsolved than solved problems. Yet from time to time we must try to take another step forward towards unravelling the mysteries of cerebral mechanisms.

A more recent discussion of the subject is given in a lecture reported in paper 19 (Russell 1968).

The development during the past two decades of what is generally referred to as molecular biology has influenced to a startling extent a great many biological sciences. The main concern of these studies has been with the nucleic acids, and virologists have led the way in many aspects of this work.

As Schmitt (1966) recently explained, these investigations have been chiefly concerned with a study of cellular and subcellular interaction by which genetic or immunological information can be stored, transferred and read out or retrieved in macromolecular DNA, RNA and protein polymers.

The importance of these advances to the neurological and psychological sciences depends on the widely held view that these new genetic and immunological dis-coveries may provide important clues with regard to the processes involved in memory in the neurological sense.

Every cell contains and maintains a genetic code for the whole body, part of which under certain circumstances transmits the structure and functions of the cells in each organ or part of an organ. These are intricate and precise methods of transferring information and therefore in one sense constitute a type of biological memory.

From the point of view of neurology there are two special aspects of this know-ledge of genetic coding. The first is concerned with the elucidation of disorders of nerve cell metabolism whether inherited or acquired. These faults in cell metabolism may result respectively in a failure of normal brain activity to develop after birth, or in later life the brain mechanisms may degenerate and thus lead to a progressive dementia. Conditions such as phenylketonuria, amaurotic family idiocy, mongolism and Huntington's chorea are relevant to these problems. The second aspect of this new knowledge is concerned intimately with the normal physiology of nerve cells and requires attention in detail, for this is our chief concern here.

As Melton (1963) has emphasized, the problems of memory have in the past lacked an interdisciplinary research interest, but things have changed greatly and the students of molecular biology, biochemistry, neurophysiology and psychology are busy trying to understand each other's language.

The normal physiology of nerve cells is concerned with many activities. One of these is the transmission of 'all or nothing' impulses conveying information over a distance. Another type of activity occurs at either end of the neurone where, on the one hand, impulses arise in the somadendrite-initial segment and, on the other, impulses are transformed by synaptic transmission into post-synaptic potentials. These post-synaptic potentials, either excitatory or inhibitory, differ in most of their characteristics from the all or nothing impulse which serves as their intermediary. For instance, they are graded with variable amplitudes and signs so that, in some cases at least, whether or not an impulse fires off down the nerve depends on the spatial and temporal integration or algebraic summation of these slower potentials. These areas at either end of the neurone are, most probably, important sites of plasticity and learning in the nervous system. Disuse, for example, has been shown to decrease the ease of transmission through the affected synapses and tetanization to facilitate transmission through disused and, to a lesser extent, normal synapses. These changes persist for seconds, minutes and perhaps hours. Such a time course, though extremely long from the physiologist's viewpoint, is much briefer than neuro-logists and psychologists usually deal with. Another example of plasticity is illustrated by experimental chromatolysis of anterior horn cells which results, not only in the classical 'structural' changes in RNA, but also in striking functional changes in thresholds of dendrite and initial segment membranes. Thereupon a previously simple monosynaptic reflex assumes a complex polysynaptic appearance. Theoreti-cally at least, less dramatic changes in RNA metabolism effected by other means may be associated with equally significant functional changes. The changes in firing of a single neurone are but part of changes in patterns of firing of populations of neurones, but physiology has not yet been as successful in studying populations and natural patterns as it has in the study of single neurones and their responses to artificially produced highly synchronous patterns of afferent bombardment. It seems fair, therefore, to say that the physiology of highly complex and patterned activity as well as that of long-term C.N.S. changes, both crucially important in any discussion of memory, have yet to be elucidated.

The problems regarding the physiology of memory and learning have recently become a centre of interest following suggestions that the coding capacity of RNA may play an important part in the story.

Thus Hydén (1966), who has led this field of thought since 1959, proposes a memory hypothesis based on the capacity for nerve cells to synthesize RNA and protein. A new form of RNA with a base sequence would be coded to correspond to the pattern of electrical activity reaching the cell.

It has also been argued that the patterns of behaviour transmitted by the chromosomes might be similar to the memory evident after learning and experience. Fairly complex behavioural patterns can certainly be inherited and therefore coded in the DNA, but the genetic mechanisms seem to operate more by influencing the pattern and growth of neural mechanisms than by anything comparable to the effects of learning and experience. Further, as Richter (1966) has emphasized, such neuronal differentiation takes place relatively slowly and thus offers no parallel to the almost instant capacity to recall a visual image or a motor skill.

It is reasonable to consider that the special metabolism of the nerve cell which has been demonstrated might be entirely required for, and concerned with, the unique capacity of the nerve cell to maintain an irritable membrane which can be depolarized at a great variety of speeds up to hundreds of times a second. The transfer of normal or abnormal characteristics through the genetic code may certainly in itself be looked on as a type of memory, but one which is very different from the plastic changes which must take place in brain cells in relation to the development of patterns of behaviour and of learning.

It seems that neuronal activity is associated with a rapidly changing production of proteins with the RNA as an activator, so that activity of any one part of the brain leads to a demonstrable increase in RNA activity.

When first made aware of this field of research and the suggestions regarding memory and learning, the general theme seemed to be unattractive, for the early ideas suggested complex information being stored in single cells—a conception which is very foreign to current views which insist that even the simplest aspect of brain activity involves a vast number of interconnecting units. However, if through the complex capacities of RNA coding a pattern of afferents arriving at the cell could be selected to determine the neurone's reaction as regards speed of discharge and timing of response, then this would be most exciting and we might really begin to understand how the C.N.S. works.

Here it may be helpful to refer to some of what is known about memory mechanisms in relation to the nervous system. It is perhaps necessary to reiterate that the activity of a nerve cell leads to repetitive discharges through its axon which generally pass to activate one or more other nerve cells. The strength of neuronal activity is based largely on the frequency of discharges via its axon. Even when apparently at rest the nerve cell may discharge spontaneously from time to time. This is a point of great theoretical interest, for the spontaneous unconscious discharge of neurones throughout life may play a part in maintaining patterns of communication between cells and may thus help to maintain memories.

If we consider, for example, the effects of a simple visual experience, this seems to activate a vast number of neurones in the brain at a very high repetitive rate of discharge over a considerable period; and this process in the trained brain involves complex grades of recognition and comparisons with previous visual experiences. There is also an emotional association of, say, pleasure or fear according also to previous experience: high arousal may facilitate learning, as measured by delayed recall experiments (Kleinsmith and Kaplan, 1963). Even if the new experience is of no interest, it is generally held and can therefore be recalled for a few seconds, but then, in the absence of any special alerting activity, it begins to fade quickly. However, if the visual experience caused sufficient alerting to encourage remembering for say, a few hours, then it seems that a repetitive process is set in operation which with the passage of time establishes a memory trace which can often be recalled perhaps a week or more later. There is now abundant evidence that there must be an unconscious ongoing process of establishing a memory which is a very vital aspect of the process. This is put out of action very promptly in its earliest stages if the brain is inactivated by cerebral concussion or by electric convulsion occurring within a few seconds of the visual experience. As the minutes pass, the memory becomes more firmly established but even after some hours the recently established memory is relatively vulnerable to cerebral insult. The entirely unconscious progressive establishment of a memory is sometimes thought of as depending on a reverberating circuit of communication between millions of neurones repeating the pattern of activity stimulated by the visual experience, and maintained on the basis of a short-term neural change (Milner, 1957).

The clinical study of retrograde amnesia (R.A.) in relation to cerebral concussion provides adequate proof of the importance of the time factor in relation to the development of a memory trace (Russell and Newcombe, 1966), and these observations are fully supported by observing the occurrence of similar periods of R.A. in relation to electroshock therapy (Williams, 1950) and also in relation to the development of Korsakoff's syndrome in which a long period of R.A. is a constant finding.

The time factor concerned with establishing a memory trace has been studied in animals by administering electroshock at various intervals after training runs. Several studies have demonstrated interference with learning on recall, if shocks are given within 10 seconds of the event to be recalled (Gerard, 1961). It seems likely, therefore, that the process of consolidation is impaired by the E.C.T. *per se*, and conversely that the neural changes necessary for learning may require to develop over a period of time.

There are also many observations regarding the relative vulnerability of recent memories and the great strength of some remote memories. These observations have been made during and after recovery from severe head injuries (Russell, 1959), and also in relation to the deteriorations of old age (Welford, 1958).

This capacity to add to the memory store only operates, however, if primitive structures in the temporal lobes of the brain and diencephalon (in the limbic system) are in a healthy state. When these are diseased, as in Korsakoff's syndrome (v.i.), new memories cannot be formed. Recent knowledge regarding the activating effects of the reticular formation of the brain stem have taught us to think of one part of the brain influencing the behaviour of another, and it looks as though the limbic system plays an essential role in enabling other parts of the brain to store new information.

The reason for repeating to you these well-established features of the simplest type of remembering is to emphasize again the vast system of intercellular communication which is involved in a very simple item of C.N.S. activity. It seems possible that this system repeats over and over again until some change takes place which establishes the original visual pattern so strongly that it becomes available for immediate recall and for innumerable correlations with future visual information arising for analysis.

In general, the capacity to develop this simple memory is thought to depend on repetitive activity, which is probably maintained by minor physico-chemical changes at synapses which depend on activity resulting in a lower threshold. These changes strengthen as the minutes and hours pass and on this basis it is easy to understand the relative vulnerability of recent memory after concussion or convulsive therapy. However, this process works better if there are no distractions after the material to be remembered. Many of you will know from experience that reading before sleep is an aid to learning and there are many psychological studies concerned with the interference with memory by brain activity following the episode to be retained. It has also been reported that sensory deprivation may improve the retention and recall of learned material (Grissom, Snedfeld and Vernon, 1962).

Further, an event that is unique in one's experience is relatively easy to remember, but if the unique event subsequently becomes common-place, then the original occurrence (once unique) may become lost to recall.

In order to study the physiology of memory and learning it is probably best to confine one's attention to some simple facet of this fundamental capacity, and therefore it is with hesitation that I continue to refer to some other aspects of memory lest these may confuse the issue by their irrelevance. However, it is wise to have some idea of the complexities we have to deal with.

The first of these is concerned with the way in which a trained brain can suddenly be alerted by a highly complex combination of circumstances. The exhausted mother who is wakened only by the cry of her child is a remarkable example, as is the reaction of the watch-dog to an unfamiliar footstep; or the experimental subject, in selective attention experiments, who normally can ignore the second channel is nevertheless able to perceive certain signals in it, for example his own name, with lowered thresholds (Treisman, 1964). As individuals we are all to a variable degree liable to be suddenly roused to anger or apprehension by a highly complex series of occurrences. Nowadays we may say this is due to the alerting effects of the reticular formation in the brain stem, but the point is that the circumstances of alerting are so complex in relation to previous experience and learning that they must require the complexities of the cerebral hemispheres for their recognition. Thus, there must be a mechanism highly facilitated whereby complex associations in the C.N.S. can jump quickly to alert the whole mechanism—a hot line to the reticular formation!

The next point which requires discussion is concerned with Korsakoff's syndrome, for this remarkable condition illustrates some important characteristics of remote memory. In this syndrome all capacity to add new information to the memory store seems to be lost. Immediate repetition of a series of digits is possible, but within 10 minutes there is no recollection of the digits, of the test being done, or of the examiner even having been seen before. This syndrome develops in relation to some very precise anatomical defects developing in the brain, all of which are

6

concerned with bilateral involvement of the limbic system. Thus, disease or excision of the hippocampus in both temporal lobes (Milner and Penfield, 1956), of the corporal mamillaria, of the medical dorsal nucleus of the thalamus (Adams, Collins and Victor, 1962), or of structures near the third ventricle (Williams and Penny-backer, 1954; Victor and Yakovlev, 1955) all produce Korsakoff's syndrome. This condition can only be studied properly in the adult (trained) brain and in such cases there is often a remarkable preservation of remote memories, skills and intellectual abilities which were developed before the illness or injury. As Talland (1965) pointed out, *time sense* in these patients has lost its cues; initiative is lacking, and there is a failure to activate and sustain a search for the retrieval of memories. As the last memories to be recalled are of events which occurred some months before the illness or injury (owing to the retrograde amnesia), it is inevitable that attempts to converse about current affairs are confused, repetitive and involved in confabulation. The most startling variety of this syndrome is that which occurs in tuberculous meningitis, for here a Korsakoff state may continue for months or even years (Williams and Smith, 1954), and yet after cure of the meningitis a good recovery of the capacity to learn may occur although of course there remains amnesia for the whole illness.

It is, of course, highly significant that during this amnesic state the remote memories which can be readily recalled were established with the aid of the limbic system which is now out of action or destroyed—hence the conception of the limbic system as driving the rest of the C.N.S. to hold information, and also the view that old memories are maintained by well-developed structural changes in many parts of the cerebrum remote from the limbic system.

There is a complexity here, for the physiology of recalling is highly obscure and yet this is also concerned somehow or other with temporal lobe function. Recalling not only involves remembering a previous event but also a strong sensation of familiarity which enables the individual to recognize the right answer. The *déjà vu* sensation of the temporal lobe fit caricatures this function while the artificially induced hallucination on temporal lobe stimulation illustrates a distorted recalling phenomenon. However, in Korsakoff's syndrome recalling of remote events may be remarkably accurate and it is not at all clear how this can happen after temporal lobe excision. However, the patient lacks the normal sense of correctness of familiarity in relation to what he remembers, for he may insist very vehemently that his con-fabulations are as true as his true memories.

Bickford and his associates (1958) have reported that stimulation of the temporal lobes (as a prelude to surgical excision), provoked a reversible retrograde amnesia. The stimulation thus appeared to affect the retrieval, rather than the consolidation process; and the retrograde amnesia was shown to be a function of the length of stimulation, covering a wide time scale, from 1 second to several weeks. These observations are comparable to the shrinkage of R.A. during recovery from cerebral concussion, for much of the R.A. first observed recovers, leaving a short period for which the R.A. is permanent. There is therefore a storing and also recalling system which are closely linked and yet are also in some respects independent: this is a very mysterious aspect of our subject.

These, then, are a very few of the observations being made on the various factors which influence memory and learning, and there is little doubt that great advances in the understanding of these problems will follow before long.

In conclusion I should like to emphasize some aspects of the problem.

(1) From the point of view of neurophysiology an experience which continues for a second or two allows time for many hundreds of repetitive neuronal discharges.

(2) These start a process which in the course of some minutes may establish a firm memory trace which holds some of the original experience for future recall.

(3) Shortly after this process starts, the receiving areas used are 'cleared' for the reception of new information, so the consolidating process is not maintained by the receiving cells.

(4) The so-called on-going process of consolidation occurs unconsciously and if allowed to continue undisturbed in a healthy brain will within a few minutes establish a memory trace which is resistant to electroshock, cerebral concussion or hypothermia.

(5) During this period of consolidation, some physical changes must operate in relation presumably to the neuronal networks involved in relation to the original experience.

(6) This pattern could presumably be maintained by repetitions from spontaneous neuronal activity, and this might cause physico-chemical changes at synapses which would allow a pattern to be resumed after interruption by, say, hypothermia.

(7) It is tempting to consider the earlier processes of establishing an engram to be physical, and that at some stage of the process the molecular biology of the nerve cell bodies should take control, but there is a grading in the vulnerability of memories which seems to stretch out (back) indefinitely through the years so that we must, I think, look for one mechanism for all stages of consolidation, or if there are two mechanisms, they must be mutually interdependent.

(8) If an original experience involves a vast number of neurones, it seems probable that the recall of that experience will activate many of the same neurones. This means that a particular pattern of interneuronal communication must be maintained through the years for every memory whether important or trifling, but presumably one cell may be involved in many different memories.

(9) This conception demands detailed discrimination by nerve cells so that they can discharge differently according to the pattern of afferent excitatory or inhibitory influences.

(10) It is beginning to look as though this discrimination must be laid down by experience in the molecules of the nerve cell body, and the question is whether the synthesis perhaps of a particular protein in the nerve cell during consolidation of learning could determine the future reactivity of the cell in such a way as to preserve a particular threshold.

Man always applies his latest discovery to the understanding of obscure problems. Ancient man may have thought of memory as an impression like seal on wax. Tubes of vital spirits were a later conception, while in more recent times electrical currents, switching points and telephone wires dominated thought.

With computers the analogy became more complex, certainly more realistic, and the science of kybernetics has developed rapidly. Now this latest analogy is with the genetic information storage and transfer-mechanisms which have been unravelled in recent years.

As time passes and further research work develops, these ideas will all be seen in a different perspective. Young (1966) has explained the great difficulties in accepting Hydén's early ideas in 1960, but if his suggestions on modifications of RNA in relation to learning can somehow be married to the vast conceptions of the students of kybernetics, then indeed I think we may take an important step forward.

I am indebted to Mrs. Freda Newcombe, D.PHIL, and Dr. Robert Young for assistance in preparing this paper.

7

FURTHER COMMENTS AND SUGGESTIONS

THE earliest of these studies were presented as a thesis for the degree of Doctor of Medicine at Edinburgh University. The 200 patients examined brought to light various problems regarding the mechanisms of concussion and of *contre-coup* which were at variance with much of the teaching of the time (the early 1930s). The duration of disturbed consciousness (referred to in later years as R.A. and P.T.A.) emerged as a useful means of classification in relation to the severity of the general cerebral commotion, and the effect of age was also found to be noteworthy.

The Second World War brought many neurologists together in 1940 at the Military Hospital for Head Injuries in Oxford and a period of intensive and profitable study of head-injury problems ensued that has been continued in Oxford ever since. The basic conception of acceleration concussion was established by experiment and confirmed from many differing points of view. The significance of the traumatic amnesias was established as a guide of practical value and treatment and rehabilitation of post-concussional patients was pursued with vigour and success.

It was late in the war that cases of missile wounds of the brain appeared in large numbers and research interests changed to a study of focal brain lesions. However, the problems of the traumatic amnesias were always to the fore and the strange occurrence of shrinking R.A., the very long R.A., and the traumatic Korsakoff syndrome were much studied.

Following the Second World War the accumulated wealth of head-injury material successfully tempted the author to abandon his appointments in Edinburgh, to settle in Oxford, and to continue working for the Army and the Ministry of Pensions. With encouragement and help from Professor Hugh Cairns and support from the Nuffield Provincial Hospitals Trust, the author and his colleagues also engaged in establishing a neurological civilian service in Oxford.

Against this background, work on pensioners with head wounds continued and collaboration with many psychologists engaging in research has been maintained. The most significant development of this period was the rapid discovery that the hippocampal regions of the temporal lobes are not a part of the olfactory system but are intimately associated with all aspects of memory and recall. This dramatic change necessitated a reappraisal of the significance of the traumatic amnesias with special reference to the time required to establish a memory trace and the vulnerability of memory traces in relation to the age of the memory.

The formation of a 'memory trace' came to be viewed as an on-going process which is effective only if the brain is healthy for at least a period of a few seconds after the event. Further, the formation of a memory that can be recalled later is prevented when there is severe bilateral disease or destruction of the limbic system.

The amnesia for periods of confusion due to disease or injury (P.T.A.) requires no special explanation as recovery of the capacity to remember seems to depend simply on a particular grade of recovery when awareness of the sequence of events can be maintained and orientation re-established. However, there is now plenty of evidence that small lesions of the limbic system (bilateral) have a very special capacity to inactivate memory-forming mechanisms although the *immediate* ability to recall is remarkably preserved.

There is naturally a tendency to correlate impairment of the on-going process of remembering (as demonstrated by the phenomenon of R.A.) with the failure to store new information in Korsakoff's syndrome due to disease of the limbic system. Clearly, memories are not stored in the limbic system, so the idea arises that the limbic system must 'drive' other parts of the brain to establish memories along with vast patterns of association that seem to occur with a forceful type of memory-stimulant.

The on-going effect of, say, a visual experience is well illustrated by the effect sometimes of looking at a television play in the evening. Later the same evening, while one is nearly asleep, scenes from the television pro-gramme, even when of no interest, may obtrude themselves to delay slum-ber. This happens even when other events following the TV programme might have been expected to remove all encouragement to the remembering process.

A particularly puzzling aspect of the problem is the connection between forming a memory and subsequently being able to recall this. If, as seems possible, a healthy limbic system drives the formation of memories throughout life, then it seems that some closely related system is required to initiate the recalling system, or could it be the same system in reverse? Recalling may depend on the activation of associations related to the original traces: on this hypothesis the initiative for recalling would come from memory stores throughout the brain and would reactivate the limbic system to drive recalling processes for long-established cortical engrams: this might form a powerful type of circuitry that is a feature of full awareness and con-sciousness.

One reason for considering that memory-formation and memory-recalling mechanisms must be, to some extent, one and the same is that during periods of failure to memorize there may be, for a short period, an R.A. extending for a period of years, and the two defects recover simultaneously, as in the 'transient global amnesia syndrome'.

Such a conception gives no explanation for the patient with a destructive temporal lobe encephalitis who can remember nothing for more than a period of about 60 seconds, has a dense R.A. for a matter of years, and yet seems to retain the skills and knowledge of language learned in earlier years. Further, he can describe accurately events prior to the onset of his R.A.

Here we must face the problem of different classes of memory system. The patient who is grossly confused remembers how to speak and how to walk, and it seems that the psychological varieties of remembering that survive for periods of years may become so firmly established that, as with a knowledge of words and simple motor skills, they are still available for use when limbic system structures are out of action.

Another feature of the limbic system activity is its apparent potentiation by emotional influences, for when these are inactivated, as in Korsakoff's psychosis, the patient seems to lose initiative and becomes emotionally flat and indifferent.

This 'emotional' aspect of the problems draws attention to the normal phenomenon of recognizing the correctness of what is recalled. This seems to be a very vital part of remembering that is caricatured by the intense feeling of familiarity experienced in some temporal lobe fits. The patient who is confused and disorientated seems to lose this and when questioned about the date follows his grossly inaccurate replies with the question 'Isn't it?' He seems to have lost all sense of recognizing which recollection is correct.

Another puzzling aspect of normal remembering is the remarkable capacity (to some extent at least) for localizing in time the event recalled, and for arranging a sequence of events with some accuracy. The establishment or the learning of a particular sequence of events is of course a basic feature of C.N.S. activity. For example, in the case of a learned motor skill there is a startling and almost incredible ability to learn sensori-motor patterns in which each of the scores of muscles involved learn to act (apparently automatically) in a precise order and controlled strength over a complicated and prolonged sequence. The skills involved in singing a song, playing the piano, or throwing a ball, are all examples of such complex sequential achievements.

The establishment and performance of such skills involves a process of learning and memory in the physiological sense, and such skills as are of long standing are usually preserved in the Korsakoff syndrome. In other words, the timing of the sensori-motor mechanisms is not directly disordered by the lesions that cause Korsakoff's syndrome. Indeed, as is well known, the lesion that destroys the memory of a motor skill is the lesion that causes apraxia, which is far removed from the limbic system structures.

As far as the hippocampus is observed, Milner, Corkin, and Teuber (1968) and Starr and Phillips (1970) have demonstrated that this part of the limbic system is particularly concerned with the memory and learning of verbal material, and that patients with bilateral destruction of most of the hippocampus can learn skills unassociated with language, such as motor skills or a musical sequence. There are therefore many unsolved problems, but the impression grows that there are a number of very active regions of the brain that continually influence or control the thresholds and performance of other areas.

The extraordinary capacity of a healthy brain to time its response to an accurate sequence has already been referred to, and this brings forward another possible factor in relation to the physiological explanation of R.A. This depends on the reasonable suggestion that any perceived event to be stored for future use must be fitted into a sequence of events both before *and after* the event. On the basis of this hypothesis the explanation of the R.A. phenomenon would depend not only on the decay of the memory trace owing to the lack of continuity of normal driving mechanisms (after concussion), but also to the blocking of events following the concussion with which the pre-accident embryo memory traces could be linked.

On a somewhat comparable approach, the important phenomenon of the transient long R.A. may be related to the probability that as man matures and as age advances, the processes of his learning and remembering become ever more complex owing to the need to fit in new information into the existing store and in the right place and context. On the basis of this hypothesis the relative vulnerability of recent memories might simply reflect an age-determined complexity of the neuronal mechanisms in the more recent memory activities. This theory would also partly explain the clear influence of age on the average duration of R.A. and P.T.A.

Thus on theoretic grounds one might expect that the long R.A. demonstrated during transient amnesic episodes occurs especially in those who have well-trained brains, and thus the 'absent-minded' professor is particularly liable to develop amnesic phenomena not only because of his age but also as a consequence of the complexity of his thought processes which render the associated neuronal organization correspondingly vulnerable to small brain lesions or to concussion.

It may be suggested therefore that the effect of age on the vulnerability of memory processes to trauma and to other insults, deserves more study especially during the earlier decades of life.

All C.N.S. activity therefore seems to be concerned with establishing patterns of response which are repeated endlessly but are, in health, amenable to modification by the further influences of the afferent streams of 'information'. It seems likely that the hippocampal part of the limbic system is specially developed in man for the activation and maintenance of the complex 'higher cerebral functions'. The anatomical aspects of its powerful influence are not at all clear but are being studied intensively.

The next chapter therefore in this complicated story is likely to come from the research neurophysiologists who are busily engaged in studying the behaviour of the cells in these structures of special interest, such as the hippocampus and amygdala. This work is already advancing rapidly and will be watched closely and with hopeful expectancy by those who think about brain mechanisms.

REFERENCES

ADAMS, R. D., COLLINS, G. H. and VICTOR, M. (1962). In *Physiologie de l'hippocampe*, p. 273. Series Colloques Internationaux, No. 107. Paris.

BANNISTER, H. and ZANGWILL, O. L. (1941). *Br. J. Psychol.* **30**, 32.

BENDER, M. B. (1956). Syndrome of isolated episode of confusion with amnesia. *J. Hillside Hospital* **5**, 212.

BICKFORD, R., MULDER, D. W., DODGE, H. W., SVIEN, H. S., and ROME, H. P. (1958). Brain and human behaviour. *Res. Publs Ass. Res. nerv. ment. Dis.* **36**, 227.

BOK, S. T. (1956). The synapses in the cerebral cortex. *Proc.1st Int. Meeting Neurologists, Amsterdam.*

BRAIN, W. R. (1950). The cerebral basis of consciousness. *Brain* **73**, 465.

BROCK, S. (1960). *Injuries of the brain and spinal cord and their coverings*, 4th edn. Springer, New York.

BURTON, H. L. (1931). *Proc. R. Soc. Med.* **24**, 1405.

DELAY, J. (1949). *Les maladies de la mémoire.* P.U.F. edn, Paris.

DENNY-BROWN, D. (1941). *Lancet* **1**, 371.

— and RUSSELL, W. R. (1941). Experimental cerebral concussion. *Brain* **64**, 93.

DEWHURST, K. and PEARSON, J. (1955). Visual hallucinations of the self in organic disease. *J. Neurol. Neurosurg. Psychiat.* **18**, 53.

ECCLES, J. C. (1953). *The neurophysiological basis of mind.* Clarendon Press, Oxford.

GERARD, R. W. (1961). In *Brain mechanisms and learning*, pp. 29 and 183. Blackwell, Oxford.

GRANIT, R. A. (1955). *Receptors and sensory perception.* Yale University Press, New Haven, Conn.

GREENFIELD, J. G. (1938) *Proc. Roy Soc. Med.* **32**, 43.

GRISSOM, R. J., SNEDFELD, P., and VERNON, J. (1962). *Science, N.Y.* **138**, 429.

HEAD, H. (1926). *Aphasia and kindred disorders of speech.* Macmillan, New York.

HOLBOURN, A. H. S. (1943). Mechanics of head injuries. *Lancet* **2**, 438.

HOOPER, R. S., McGREGOR, J. M., and NATHAN, P. W. (1945). *J. ment. Sci.* **91**, 458.

HUMPHREY, M. E. and ZANGWILL, O. L. (1951). Cessation of dreaming after brain injury. *J. Neurol. Neurosurg. Psychiat.* **14**, 322.

HYDÉN, H. (1966). In *Neurosciences research symposium*, Vol. 1. M.I.T. Press, Cambridge, Mass.

JACKSON, J. H. (1874). *Selected writings of John Hughlings Jackson* (ed. J. Taylor). Hodder and Stoughton, London 1932.

JEFFERSON, G. (1942). *Glasg. med. J.* **20**, 77.

KLEINSMITH, L. J. and KAPLAN, S. (1963). *J. exp. Psychol.* **65**, 190.

MELTON, A. W. (1963). Implications of short-term memory for a general theory of memory. *J. verb. Learning verb. Behaviour* **2**, 1.

MILNER, B. and PENFIELD, W. (1956). *Trans. Am. neurol. Ass.* **42**,

— CORKIN, S. and TEUBER, H. L. (1968). Further analysis of the hippocampal amnesic syndrome: 14-year follow-up study of H. M. *Neuropsychologia* **6**, 215.

MILNER, P. M. (1957). *Psychol. Rev.* **64**, 242.

MUMENTHALER, M. and VON ROLL, L. (1969). Amnestische Episoden. *Schweiz. med. Wschr.* **99**, 133.

OPPENHEIMER, D. R. (1968). Microscopic lesions in the brain following head injury. *J. Neurol. Neurosurg. Psychiat.* **31**, 299.

PUDENZ, R. H. and SHELDON, C. W. (1946). The lucite Calvarium. 3. Cranial trauma and brain movement. *J. Neurosurg.* **3**, 487.

RENSHAW, B. (1946). *J. Neurophysiol.* **9**, 191.

RICHTER, D., ed. (1966). *Aspects of learning and memory.* Heinemann, London.

ROBINSON, P. K. and WATT, A. C. (1947). *Brain* **70**, 440.

ROUGHHEAD, W. (1929). *The trial of John Donald Merritt.* Edinburgh.

RUSSELL, W. RITCHIE (1932). Cerebral involvement in head injury. *Brain* **55**, 549.

— (1934). The after-effects of head injury. *Edinb. med. J.* **41**, 129.

— (1935). Amnesia following head injuries. *Lancet* **2**, 762.

— (1947). The anatomy of traumatic epilepsy. *Brain* **70**, 225

— (1948a). Traumatic amnesia. *Q. J. exp. Psychol.* **1**, 1.

— (1948b). Studies in amnesia. *Edinb. med. J.* **55**, 92.

— (1951). Disability caused by brain wounds. *J. Neurol. Neurosurg. Psychiat.* **14**, 35.

— (1958). The physiology of memory. *Proc. R. Soc. Med.* **5i**, 9.

— (1959). *Brain: memory: learning.* Clarendon Press, Oxford.

— (1963). Amnésie de mémoration caused by brain wounds. *Trans. Am. neurol. Ass.* pp. 43–44.

— (1968). *Biochemical aspects of neurological disorders,* 3rd series, Chapter 11, pp. 155–64. Blackwell Scientific Publications, Oxford.

— and NATHAN, P. W. (1946). Traumatic amnesia. *Brain* **69**, 280.

— and NEWCOMBE, F. (1966). In *Aspects of learning and memory.* (ed. D. Richter). Heinemann, London.

— and SCHILLER, F. (1949). Crushing injuries to the skull: clinical and experimental observations. *J. Neurol. Neurosurg. Psychiat.* **12**, 52.

— and SMITH, AARON (1961). Post-traumatic amnesia in closed head injury. *Archs Neurol., Chicago* **5**, 4.

— and SPALDING, J. M. K. (1950). Treatment of painful amputation stumps. *Br. med. J.* **2**, 68.

— and WHITTY, C. W. M. (1955). Studies in traumatic epilepsy: 3 visual fits. *J. Neurol. Neurosurg. Psychiat.* **18**, 79.

SCHMITT, F. O. (1966). In *Neurosciences research symposium summaries,* Vol. I. M.I.T. Press, Cambridge, Mass.

SCOVILLE, W. B. and MILNER, B. (1957). Loss of recent memory after bilateral hippocampal lesions. *J. Neurol. Neurosurg. Psychiat.* **20**, 11.

SOMERVILLE, C. W. (1931). *Edinb. med. J.* **38**, No. 8.

STARR, ARNOLD and PHILLIPS, LAURA (1970). Verbal and motor memory in the amnestic syndrome. *Neuropsychologia* **8**, 75.

STRICH, S. J. (1956). Diffuse degeneration of the cerebral white matter in severe dementia following head injury. *J. Neurol. Neurosurg. Psychiat.* **19**, 163.

SYMONDS, C. P. (1932). *Lancet* **1**, 820.

— and RUSSELL, W. RITCHIE (1943). Accidental head injuries. *Lancet* **1**, 7.

TALLAND, G. A. (1965). *Deranged memory.* Academic Press, London.

TREISMAN, A. M. (1964). *Am. J. Psychol.* **77**, 533.

TROTTER, W. (1924). *Lancet* **1**, 935.

VICTOR, M. and YAKOVLEV, P. I. (1955). *Neurology, Minneap.* **5**, 394.

WELFORD, A. T. (1958). *Ageing and human skill.* Oxford University Press for the Nuffield Foundation.

WILLIAMS, M. (1950). *J. Neurol. Neurosurg. Psychiat.* **13**, 30.

— and SMITH, H. V. (1954). *J. Neurol. Neurosurg. Psychiat.* **17**, 173.

— and PENNYBACKER, J. (1954). *J. Neurol. Neurosurg. Psychiat.* **17**, 115.

YOUNG, J. Z. (1946). *Patterns of substance and activity in the nervous system.* H. K. Lewis, London.

— (1966). *The memory system of the brain.* Clarendon Press, Oxford.

AUTHOR INDEX

ADAMS, R. D., 72

BANNISTER, H., 18
BENDER, M. B., 49
BICKFORD, R., 72
BOK, S. T., 61
BRAIN, W. R., 63
BROCK, S., 31
BURTON, H. L., 44

COLLINS, G. H., 72
CORKIN, S., 76

DELAY, J., 57
DENNY-BROWN, D., 21, 50
DEWHURST, K., 65
DODGE, H. W., 72

ECCLES, J. C., 60, 61

GERARD, R. W., 57, 70
GRANIT, R. A., 60
GREENFIELD, J. G., 17
GRISSOM, R. J., 71

HEAD, H., 30
HOLBOURN, A. H. S., 30
HOOPER, R. S., 45
HUMPHREY, M. E., 64
HYDÉN, H., 69, 73

JACKSON, J. H., 30
JEFFERSON, G., 17

KAPLAN, S., 70
KLEINSMITH, L. J., 70

LEWIN, W. S., 27

McGREGOR, J. M., 45
MELTON, A. W., 68
MILNER, B., 63, 72, 76
MILNER, P. M., 70
MULDER, D. W., 72
MUMENTHALER, M., 49

NATHAN, P. W., 15 f., 35, 45, 65
NEWCOMBE, F., 70

OPPENHEIMER, D. R., 1, 33, 34

PEARSON, J., 65
PENFIELD, W., 67, 72
PENNYBACKER, J. B., 72
PHILLIPS, L., 76
PUDENZ, R. H., 30, 50

RENSHAW, B., 67
RICHTER, D., 69
ROBINSON, P. K., 64
ROME, H. P., 72
ROUGHHEAD, W., 47

SCHILLER, F., 50
SCHMITT, F. O., 68
SCOVILLE, W. B., 63
SHELDON, C. W., 30, 50
SMITH, AARON, 20 ff.
SMITH, H. V., 48, 72
SNEDFIELD, P., 71
SOMERVILLE, C. W., 46
SPALDING, J. M. K., 63
STARR, A., 76
STRICH, S. J., 1, 32, 33
SVIEN, H. S., 72
SYMONDS, C. P., 8, 12, 17, 24

TALLAND, G. A., 72
TEUBER, H. L., 72
TREISMAN, A. M., 71
TROTTER, W., 4

VERNON, J., 71
VICTOR, M., 71, 72
VON ROLL, L., 49

WATT, A. C., 64
WELFORD, A. T., 70
WHITTY, C. W. M., 64
WILLIAMS, M., 70, 72

YAKOVLEV, P. I., 72
YOUNG, J. Z., 60, 73

ZANGWILL, O. L., 18, 64

SUBJECT INDEX